Listen!
GOD
IS SPEAKING
TO YOU

LARGE-PRINT DEVOTIONS

HENRY E. PAUSTIAN

NORTHWESTERN PUBLISHING HOUSE
MILWAUKEE, WISCONSIN

Second printing, 2007
Second edition, 2005
First edition, 1992

Cover photo: ShutterStock, Inc.
Art Director: Karen Knutson
Designer: Pamela Wood

Library of Congress Control Number: 92-50172
Northwestern Publishing House
1250 N. 113th St., Milwaukee, WI 53226-3284
www.nph.net
© 1992, 2005 by Northwestern Publishing House
Published 2005
Printed in the United States of America
ISBN 978-0-8100-0431-3

CONTENTS

PREFACE

How comforting and reassuring it is when our heavenly Father speaks to us in our moments of fear or sorrow! He always provides just the message we need to hear, and quickly we find ourselves facing our problem with new hope and confidence.

In this book we hope to bring you the voice of God as he speaks to you in situations that trouble you, especially as you grow older. In these pages, we can offer only a sampling of such situations and how God so wonderfully addresses them. It is our fervent hope that these pages will open your eyes to the comfort and guidance God has to offer you in all the circumstances that may at some time touch your life. It is our hope that you will know where to look for relief. It is our hope that you will discover anew how wonderfully God speaks to you in his Word, so that you seek his voice as your first resource in every need.

Henry Paustian

1

HE SPEAKS TO YOU EVEN
WHEN HE SEEMS SILENT

Jesus did not answer a word.

— *(Matthew 15:23)* —

The world often accuses God of being silent, indifferent to the misery and suffering even of his own people. After all, he is the almighty God. Could he not with one word or with one wave of his majestic hand stamp out every form of misery? Such questions—questions we've perhaps asked ourselves too—are raised in a book with the title *The Silence of God*.

Even we who should know better are at times bothered by what we consider "the silence of God," that is, the apparent lack of a response from God when we cry to him over and over for help and there appears to be no answer. Doesn't he hear us? Doesn't he care? The woman of Canaan may have felt that way when she desperately cried to Jesus for help, and "Jesus did not answer a word." The psalmist expressed that same sort of desperate anguish with the words "I cry out by day, but you do not answer" (Psalm 22:2).

1

This very day it may seem to us too that God is silent, unwilling to speak and offer comfort for some misery of ours. But could it be that the problem is not with his not speaking but with our not hearing? Remember that in all his dealings with us, he acts in perfect wisdom and love. He always speaks what we need to hear and precisely when we need to hear it.

If for a time he is silent to our cry, his is the silence of higher thoughts and wiser purposes. Knowing him as we do, we want to react as his mother did at Cana when he gently turned aside her request with the words "My time has not yet come" (John 2:4). She wisely did not take this as a refusal. She recognized that Jesus was not turning her away. Rather, she saw in his words the promise that his hour would come, at the right time. And, of course, it did.

Through what channels does he speak to those of us who live so many years after he walked visibly among us? At times, he may use events that touch our lives to draw us closer to himself—perhaps through an accident or illness or the death of a friend. But our Lord most clearly speaks to us from the pages of his Word, that totally reliable, verbally inspired, inerrant Word of which Moses wrote, "The word is very near you; it is in your mouth and in your heart so you may obey it" (Deuteronomy 30:14). That Word is ever ready to comfort and guide and strengthen us as we read it or as we meditate on Bible verses we memorized in our childhood many years ago. We will find that he is always ready to speak to us in his Word, always having precisely the words we need.

Even when our hearing has become so impaired that our family needs to shout to get through to us, we will hear our heavenly Father speaking to us, not only offering comfort but also working that comfort in us. He not only guides us in what we should do but also gives us strength and willingness to do it. What a source of help that Word is!

The world calls the silence of God the greatest proof that he does not exist. We Christians may find it the greatest test of our faith. Although it is difficult to wait, and we usually want help now rather than at some future time, we simply need to let our faith take over and to keep listening for his voice, knowing assuredly that he will provide a special word for every situation we face. He is more anxious to speak than we are to hear. Waiting becomes easier if we remember that he is also waiting, waiting for the right time to speak to us. Confidently we can say with young Samuel, "Speak, for your servant is listening" (1 Samuel 3:10).

— *Prayer* —

At times, dear Lord, you seem so very silent, just when we most need to hear your voice. Help us to wait patiently for you to speak. Give us hearing ears and believing hearts, ready to accept whatever you would say to us. Amen.

2

HE SPEAKS TO YOU
WHO ARE SHUT-INS

*I have learned to be content
whatever the circumstances.*

— (Philippians 4:11) —

Life changes quite drastically for people when they become shut-ins. Gone are many of the pleasant experiences they once took for granted. No more travel, no more shopping, no more worship in God's house, no more anything, it seems.

In their busy years, they may have longed for just a few such quiet, inactive days away from the pressures and busy schedules of their lives. Now they would so love to take a leisurely drive, to visit a friend, to stroll through the shopping mall or even a grocery store. But all that is past. They've joined the growing army of shut-ins.

What can God say to make the burdens lighter if we are shut-ins? How can he make us into cheerful and content people? How can he keep us from becoming constant complainers, who make life miserable, not only for ourselves but for others as well? One of God's answers for such questions is found in these words of the apostle Paul: "I have learned to be content whatever the circumstances."

Paul's contentment must have been a mystery to many who knew him, for he was suffering more misery and enduring greater dangers than all of us put together. His travels took him down the road of persecution and hostility. He was beaten, stoned, shipwrecked, and imprisoned. Yet instead of being embittered and full of complaints, he was totally content, even to the point of rejoicing that he was counted worthy to suffer in the service of Jesus.

Paul was not that way by nature. He tells us that he had to learn such contentment. What taught him this amazing spirit? After years of total Pharisaic self-righteousness, Paul had learned to know himself as a hopeless, condemned sinner who could expect nothing but hell. But then Christ sought him out on that Damascene highway, and Paul came to know Christ and his love, that love of which Paul then spoke so simply and yet so eloquently: "[Christ] loved me and gave himself for me" (Galatians 2:20). That love assured Paul of the love of God from which nothing could ever separate him again.

Serving God faithfully brought Paul plenty of suffering, but he could now look at those sufferings not as angry blows from God but as tools of God, used by him to further his plans for Paul's eternal future. And when he became *a kind of shut-in* (he was imprisoned in a Roman jail cell), even this was serving God's purpose. It enabled Paul to witness to the elite prison guards and, through them, to many others in Rome.

This was but one of many happy surprises Paul experienced as God's child. Paul did not enjoy his suffering any more than we would enjoy being shut-ins, but he knew that it was necessary, for God does not permit his beloved children to suffer unnecessarily for even one moment. Nor does he allow them to experience an ounce of misery that will not serve his eternal purposes for them. So Paul was content. God was working out his purposes in Paul's life in absolute wisdom and love, and that was all Paul needed to know. His path of suffering was not an aimless detour. He could confidently exclaim with the psalmist, "You guide me with your counsel, and afterward you will take me into glory" (Psalm 73:24).

No, a child of God would not choose the life of a shut-in. But whatever may happen to us, we are grateful that we can confidently leave the control over our lives and the difficult decisions of life up to God and say, "Your way, not mine, O Lord." We can still pray for a return to a more normal life, for God has plenty of miracles left. If God decides to put that wheelchair aside, he will do just that. Whatever God chooses, the worst of suffering as shut-ins is not worthy to be compared with the glory that shall be revealed in us. Then suddenly there will be no more wheelchairs for us, or pain pills, or dimmed eyes, but only perfect peace and contentment in his presence. Until then, we can be content and wait for his purposes to unfold. They are worth waiting for!

— *Prayer* —

**We know, Lord, that whatever circumstances
you choose for us, they serve your loving purpose.
Teach us with Paul to be content. Give us
such a faith as this. Amen.**

3

HE SPEAKS TO YOU AS YOU ARE TROUBLED BY WEAKNESS

"My grace is sufficient for you, for my power is made perfect in weakness." Therefore I will boast all the more gladly about my weaknesses, so that Christ's power may rest on me. That is why, for Christ's sake, I delight in weaknesses, in insults, in hardships, in persecutions, in difficulties. For when I am weak, then I am strong.

— (2 Corinthians 12:9,10) —

If ever a person had the right to boast of his strength and accomplishments, it would have to have been the apostle Paul. He accomplished more in the Lord's service than all the other apostles combined. Yet we don't hear a word of his boasting in his own wisdom or strength. Rather, Paul gloried in his weaknesses.

How could this be, when it must have seemed that his weaknesses would certainly hinder him in the work that was so dear to him? More than that. How could this apostle actually take pleasure in his weakness? Twice he explained:

"So that Christ's power may rest on me" and "When I am weak, then I am strong."

God explains to us here how the weaknesses that pile up in life, including old age, can actually become advantages and blessings to us. Paul had some kind of "thorn in the flesh," some weakness that seemed to hinder him in his work. Three times he prayed to be delivered from it. God surely loved Paul and was even more concerned about his mission than was the apostle, yet he gently said no to Paul's repeated request. "My grace is sufficient for you, for my power is made perfect in weakness" was God's answer.

Paul understood. He writes, "I will boast all the more gladly about my weaknesses, so that Christ's power may rest on me." The power needed to accomplish his work was not his own. It was the Lord's. He added, "I delight in weaknesses, in insults, in hardships, in persecutions, in difficulties. For when I am weak, then I am strong."

Without Christ, Paul could accomplish nothing. Any wisdom or strength he had belonged to Christ. And when he learned not to trust in his own strength and ability but to rely totally on the Lord's, then the Lord could take over and great things would happen. The blind would see, the deaf would hear, sinners would become saints, the dead would live. These wonders could happen only when Paul had emptied the cup of his own wisdom and let the Lord fill it with his. So Paul says, "When I am weak, then I am strong."

How meaningful this is for us as the weaknesses of aging set in. We, like Paul, need to learn to trust totally in a strength and wisdom far greater than our own. We want to ask God to fill our cup with whatever we need to do his will.

Enlarging on the prayer of the disciples, we could pray: "Lord, we do believe, but help us in our unbelief and doubts. Lord, we do love you, but help us in our times of indifference. Lord, we do struggle against temptation, but give us more victories. Lord, we do try to follow you, but keep us from straying so often. Lord, we do try to obey, but keep us from frequent disobedience. We are weak. Lord, make us strong."

God has spoken clearly. When we empty our cup of self-reliance and go to him with that empty cup, he will gladly fill it for us, teaching us in the process that nothing really depends on us. In this spirit, a soldier once wrote, "I asked God for power that I might have the praise of men; I was given weakness that I might feel the need of God."

God cannot pour his riches into a cup that is already full, so take your *empty* cup to him. When weaknesses trouble you, say with Paul, "When I am weak, then I am strong."

— *Prayer* —

Lord, sometimes we feel so awfully weak. We wonder how we can cope with the problems of the day. May our weaknesses become blessings in disguise as they teach us to look always to you for help. May your strength be made perfect in our weaknesses. Amen.

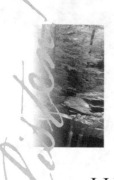

4

HE SPEAKS TO YOU WHEN YOU ARE GUILT-RIDDEN

The blood of Jesus, his Son,
purifies us from all sin.

— (1 John 1:7) —

How hopeless it would be to face life without God! How devastatingly worse it would be to face life knowing that God is against us in all that we do! If that were the case, we could feel absolutely no hope at all, only bleak despair. Paul's mighty statement: "If God is for us, who can be against us?" (Romans 8:31) would take on the opposite meaning: "If God is against us, who can be for us?"

We can all think of enough reasons why God *should* be against us. We have trampled his commandments underfoot repeatedly, rebelled against his will, and defied him in thought, word, and act—this in spite of all the mercy he has shown us. Satan whispers in our ears, and our consciences concur, that God surely is against us and will condemn us exactly as we deserve.

What an intense relief it is to know that the very one against whom we've sinned has provided us with a sure defense. That is the unmistakable message of the whole Bible. "The blood of Jesus, his Son, purifies us from all sin." Read it as though hearing the good news for the first time and consider what it means for you.

God found the one way he could remain a just God and yet not punish us sinners. His Son took our place and was punished in our stead. Jesus turned God's anger away from us, the prophet Isaiah declares, by taking it all upon himself on the cross. Describing that event as vividly in prophecy as though he himself stood at the foot of the cross, Isaiah explains that "he was pierced for our transgressions, he was crushed for our iniquities . . . and by his wounds we are healed" (Isaiah 53:5).

Jeremiah already assured the people of his day that God's thoughts toward them were no longer thoughts of anger but of peace. They had been reconciled to God by the death of his Son. When, in shame, we recall some of our own sins that seem beyond such forgiving mercy of God, he has Isaiah quiet our misgivings, "Though your sins are like scarlet, they shall be as white as snow; though they are red as crimson, they shall be like wool" (Isaiah1:18). And they are that, white as wool, forgiven. The Lamb of God has taken away the sins of the world, including ours.

How zealously God wants us to know the peace of forgiveness. Paul dares to assert that the almighty God, against whom we have sinned, actually pleads with us to be reconciled to him. "We are therefore Christ's ambassadors, as though God were making his appeal through us. We implore you on Christ's behalf: Be reconciled to God" (2 Corinthians 5:20). What incredible love and mercy!

The psalmist also found this forgiving mercy of God one of the most incredible attributes of God. Such mercy fills us with the same sense of awe and wonder that we might feel when we think of his creation might or his wisdom. It is so awesome that we can believe it only because God himself has revealed it to us and brought our hearts to accept it. And so it is that we *know* with Paul that we have peace.

Yes, we *can* speak as boldly as Paul, "If God is for us, who can be against us?" (Romans 8:31). Aging brings us closer to our own deaths, but the prospect no longer frightens us. It fills us instead with the joyous anticipation of being welcomed home by the King. Let's not carry around that unbearable burden of past sins as though Jesus failed in his mission. He himself said, "It is finished" (John 19:30). Our redemption is a fact. It is ours to turn to for comfort and peace and hope all our lives. Yes, "the blood of Jesus, his Son, purifies us from all sin."

— *Prayer* —

Savior, when our sins trouble us and feelings
of guilt overwhelm us, may we simply lift
our eyes to the cross and discover again
the peace you won for us there. Amen.

5

HE SPEAKS TO YOU ABOUT WISE PRIORITIES

"Seek first his kingdom and his righteousness, and all these things will be given to you as well."

— *(Matthew 6:33)* —

The story is told of a mischievous man who entered the display window of a large department store one night and rearranged all the price tags. In the morning shoppers were thrilled to discover that expensive, costly items were now cheap. On the other hand, the rather worthless, undesirable items all had big price tags.

Sometimes it's as though someone has, indeed, mixed up all the price tags in our lives. The sad result is that some things we value very highly are among the things that really don't count for anything, especially in the light of eternity. At the same time, we sometimes barely take a second look at the real treasures we possess: church, family, friends, Christian homes, our health—yes, even salvation and heaven.

Setting poor priorities can make a person's life miserable. So in his Sermon on the Mount, our Lord seeks to straighten out our sense of values. Instead of making it our goal in life to pursue trivialities and trash, which moth and rust corrupt and thieves steal, we are, as Jesus urges, to "seek first his kingdom and his righteousness."

We are all aware that nothing in life is as vital and precious as our place in God's kingdom and family. Sometimes, however, we suspect that if we put God and salvation first, we will lose out on some of the treasures of life that others seem to enjoy so much.

The truth is that we lose nothing and gain everything by putting God's kingdom first. "All these things will be given to you as well," the Lord promises. Putting him first does *not* cause us to lose anything of value. Rather, along with the treasures of heaven, all the earthly blessings we need will be given us too—thrown in for good measure.

By faith in Jesus, we have become the very children of God, so we simply no longer need to fret about earthly things. "Your heavenly Father knows that you need them" (Matthew 6:32). Our earthly needs are part of the Father's concern for his children. And we know that he did not even spare his own Son when we needed him to be our Savior. How then can we fear that he will not—together with this greatest of all gifts—also freely give us all the lesser things we need? They cost him nothing compared with that greatest of all gifts.

Solomon, for example, had a wise set of priorities. When God threw the gate to all his treasures wide open before Solomon and invited him to take his pick, Solomon asked the Lord for the wisdom to rule his people well. Because he did not ask for wealth or power or fame, God poured out on him such a measure of earthly goods that the whole world marveled.

Of course there are earthly pleasures that give great enjoyment, for that is God's intent when he gives them. But earthly pleasures can't compare in value with what God has given us in Christ. In a parable that Jesus told, the pearl buyer found the one perfect pearl and then gladly and joyously sold all his lesser pearls without the least bit of reluctance. He had found the very best there was. In the same manner, Moses "chose to be mistreated along with the people of God rather than to enjoy the pleasures of sin for a short time. He regarded disgrace for the sake of Christ as of greater value than the treasures of Egypt" (Hebrew 11:25,26). So the apostle Paul, having found Christ, gladly exchanged honor and wealth and ease for a life of persecution.

What are your priorities? What is more important to you, to have Christ or the things that the world counts as treasures? Remember, in Jesus you have everything you could ever need. Everything! "In him, peace," said Paul. He could have added, "In him, security; in him, joy; in him, wisdom; in him, heaven."

Christ Jesus is our priceless treasure. Jesus is our source of purest pleasure. May he be our highest priority!

— *Prayer* —

Lord, help us learn and desire more and more what is most important in life. May we always seek first the kingdom of God and his righteousness, knowing that all lesser needs will also be met for us. For Jesus' sake. Amen.

6

HE SPEAKS TO YOU
ABOUT EARTHLY NEEDS

*My God will meet all your needs according
to his glorious riches in Christ Jesus.*

— *(Philippians 4:19)* —

In the parsonage where I grew up, unexpected guests would frequently show up about suppertime. Although we always welcomed them warmly, they presented a predicament for my mother. Since she often had enough difficulty providing food for the ten of us in the family, she sometimes had to resort to prearranged signals to manage the meal. As we sat down to eat with our guests, we were made aware of a possible shortage of food with a quietly whispered signal, "FHB"—Family Hold Back! At other times, we were relieved to hear the other signal, "MIK"—More In Kitchen. Either way, we did not go hungry; the Lord saw to that.

The Lord once had a somewhat similar problem when he had five thousand men plus their families as "unexpected" guests. So eager had these people been to see Jesus perform a miracle and to hear his words that they had come out into the wilderness without bringing food along.

We all know about the miracle that took care of the problem. We want to observe closely the *way* in which Jesus dealt with this entire situation. It teaches us something about wise priorities.

Notice that he first took care of their most pressing need by bringing them the bread of life, offering them full, free forgiveness for their sins. Then he provided food for their stomachs by performing a miracle.

Jesus had not come from heaven merely to deal with earthly concerns. The intent behind all his miracles went far beyond mere material needs, healing and sight and bread. The miracles were signs pointing to Jesus as the Son of God, the Savior. All the bread in the world does not help people if they do not know him as their Lord and Savior.

In the miracle of the feeding of the five thousand, we do see that his compassion also extends to peoples' bodily hunger. John tells us that Jesus knew from the beginning what he would do, but in order to test his disciples, he asked Philip, "Where shall we buy bread for these people to eat?" (John 6:5).

Jesus' words remind us that he is well aware of our bodily needs. The miracle that followed assures us that he will take care of our material needs as well. But he would also have us keep in mind that whatever our material needs, he has already met our most urgent need in providing for us the bread of life and the forgiveness of all our sins.

All other blessings—however needed and precious—are in a sense merely the crumbs that fall from his table. He who owns the universe gives these gifts out of his abundance. Contrast all those gifts with his most precious gift, his own

Son, who was given into death for us. That gift makes us absolutely certain that he will provide for our earthy needs. That gift makes us his own, and it also makes our needs his own as our heavenly Father. As it is written, "He who did not spare his own Son, but gave him up for us all—how will he not also, along with him, graciously give us all things?" (Romans 8:32).

Paul expresses God's promise to provide for us with these words: "My God will meet all your needs according to his glorious riches in Christ Jesus." All your needs—never in a miserly way, but lavishly, abundantly, richly—will be taken care of. The lavishness of his gifts is evidenced in this, that after he had fed all those guests, and after all of them had been satisfied, more was left over than the disciples had at the start.

We all have earthly needs of one kind or another. What a comfort to have such a friend and provider, the Lord who each harvesttime, in ripe fields of grain all over the world, multiplies the miracle of the feeding of the thousands a billion times! Luther says he does this providing "richly and daily." The eyes of all wait upon him, and he gives them their food in due season. He will never leave us destitute, not ever. He will provide. He has promised us that. Trust him!

— Prayer —

Whenever earthly needs trouble us, Lord,
help us remember how simply you fed the Israelites
in the desert with manna and quail and how easily
you provided for the hungry thousands. May we bring
all our needs to you with quiet confidence and serene
trust, certain that you will never fail us. Amen.

7

HE SPEAKS TO YOU
WHEN YOU WORRY

*Cast all your anxiety on him
because he cares for you.*

— *(1 Peter 5:7)* —

We have all had the privilege of knowing people who were always cheerful and optimistic, who never seemed downcast or anxious no matter what the circumstances. How we wish that *we* could always be like that! We have probably all done more than a little worrying in our day, often about trivial things, often about situations that never did happen as we were so concerned they might.

We've all learned, in fact, that worry is not productive. It does not solve our problems. Instead, it usually creates new ones. Worry, for example, makes us nervous, tense, and irritable and can even affect our health. The psalmist took himself to task for such worrying: "Why are you downcast, O my soul? Why so disturbed within me?" (Psalm 42:5).

Yet, in spite of the fact that you know worry is counterproductive, perhaps you are struggling at this very moment with a severe problem that has you worrying. You don't like to

19

worry, I'm sure, for you know that God tells you over and over not to be fearful or anxious.

What can we remember today to help us be rid of worry? First of all, worry is hardly an expression of bold, happy trust in God and his promises. Rather, it is an indication of doubt. It gives the impression that we are not very sure about God's concern and ability always to help. Worry casts doubt on God's truth. Furthermore, worry hardly makes us effective witnesses of his grace and mercy to others, for if we who know God best are given to worry, why should those who don't know him trust him?

Worry is one of Satan's carefully chosen weapons. He seductively loves to whisper into our hearts: "Where is that God of yours? Where is that love he professes to have for you? And what about all those fine-sounding promises to protect you and provide for you?"

Knowing how God feels about worry, we would all rather live in the bold confidence of the psalmist who says: "I will trust in you. . . . I will not be afraid" (Psalm 56:3,11). We'd love to be able to say with Eli, "He is the LORD; let him do what is good in his eyes" (1 Samuel 3:18), or with Job, "Though he slay me, yet will I hope in him" (Job 13:15).

But how do we rid ourselves of this faith-destroying habit? Our patient God has much to say about worry in words that actually have the power to change worry into trust. In Philippians 4:6, he urges, "Do not be anxious about anything, but in everything, by prayer and petition, with thanksgiving, present your requests to God."

We meet worry by praying with thanksgiving, knowing right from the very beginning that God will never let us down. We can chase our worries away as did Jonah, who added to his prayer for deliverance a cry of praise even before he was delivered. We banish our worry by lifting up our eyes unto the hills, to him who made heaven and earth. We find our joyous trust once again by looking away from the wind and waves—the troubles and disturbances of life—to him who has so regularly proved his ability to deal with any crisis.

When young King Hezekiah received dire warnings from the leaders of a powerful enemy army, he simply took their threatening letter to the temple and spread it out before the Lord, as if to say, "This is your problem, Lord; I trust you." In short, he placed his problems into the Lord's hands with the firm conviction that the Lord was willing and able to take care of them.

May we reach the same conviction, that we need never worry, as expressed in the words of a favorite hymn: "Oh, what peace we often forfeit, Oh, what needless pain we bear, All because we do not carry Everything to God in prayer!" (CW 411:1).

Use God's advice for dealing with worry and anxiety, and you will be amazed at the peace that will fill your hearts. Challenge every pesky problem with one of God's sure promises. "Commit your way to the LORD; trust in him and he will do this" (Psalm 37:5).

— Prayer —

Lord, you have not only told us never to worry, but you have removed every reason to do so. May we learn to cast all our cares upon you. Amen.

8

HE SPEAKS TO YOU WHEN YOU ARE DEEPLY TROUBLED

"Be still, and know that I am God."

— *(Psalm 46:10)* —

We all have had times when life went along very smoothly, without a cloud in the sky, times when we more or less took our religion for granted. Then, with the force of an object crashing into a stone wall, some great crisis struck our lives. It might have been a sudden illness, the loss of a job, or a fire that destroyed our home. Suddenly we felt the need to take a closer look at what we believed, to reconsider the promises of God that we had trusted.

Hasn't he assured us repeatedly that he has cast our sins behind his back and forgiven them for Jesus' sake? Hasn't he promised to watch over us as his children? What is the worth of such promises now?

We urge you to sit quietly and listen when you are troubled by such thoughts. God has something to say to you: "Be still, and know that I *am* God."

Be still. You recognize that this is not the angry, disgusted voice of a frustrated mother, directed at a doubting, disobedient child. It is rather the soothing, comforting voice of a gentle mother holding a frightened child awakened out of a bad dream and whispering: "Be still. Don't be afraid. I'm right here. I won't leave you for a moment. You are safe."

As you hear these words, you are no longer afraid. For this is no longer merely the voice of some loving mother attempting to soothe your fears. The voice is that of the Lord himself, speaking to calm your troubled heart. His voice stills the fear of whatever it is that is threatening you, for you know the wonder of his love for you.

A little child once said, "I asked Jesus how much he loved me, and he spread out his arms and died." That much! We witnessed that love in action in Gethsemane, protecting his disciples. We heard it even more dramatically hours later in his prayer for the very soldiers crucifying him, "Father, forgive them, for they do not know what they are doing" (Luke 23:34). We marveled at that love displayed in the patient way he dealt with the disciples ,who deserted him, and in the way he restored Peter, who denied him.

We have experienced Christ's love in our own lives countless times and heard it reaching out to us in every word of the Bible. He speaks to our troubled faith, "A bruised reed he will not break, and a smoldering wick he will not snuff out" (Isaiah 42:3). That love reaches out to us in this invitation: "Come to me, all you who are weary and burdened, and I will give you rest" (Matthew 11:28).

We could search the whole Bible in vain to find one instance where God has failed to keep his promise. We could search our entire lives and wind up with the same results.

"Fear not," he tells us so often, and then in many instances he adds the reasons why we need never fear. In Isaiah 43:1-3, for example, he adds: "for I have redeemed you; I have summoned you by name; you are mine. When you pass through the waters, I will be with you; and when you pass through the rivers, they will not sweep over you. When you walk through the fire, you will not be burned. . . . For I am the LORD, your God."

Isn't a troubled, anxious heart in effect denying the truth of such promises, saying that maybe we can't completely trust the Lord, that maybe he doesn't care what happens to us, that possibly he is not as mighty as the needs and troubles surrounding us today?

We *do* know better than that, don't we? We've seen the love that reaches out to us from the cross. We've learned the power of his might in the biblical account of creation. We've become convinced that all our enemies and problems are in his control, that he holds the whole world in his hands, that nothing is too difficult for him. Our troubles are not the servants of Satan that will destroy us; they are servants of our Lord—servants that must serve him and us. Paul says, "We are more than conquerors through him who loved us" (Romans 8:37). We can't command our troubles to go away, as the Lord can, but we know that he will deal with them. In the meantime, he whispers in our ears, "Be still, and know that I am God."

We can rejoice with Paul, "If God is for us, who can be against us?" (Romans 8:31).

— Prayer —

Dear Lord and Savior, today we remember with comfort your words: "Do not let your hearts be troubled" (John 14:1). Give us the assurance both of your desire and of your ability to deal with all our cares. Amen.

9

HE SPEAKS TO YOU WHEN YOU ARE HOSPITALIZED

God is our refuge and strength,
an ever-present help in trouble. Therefore
we will not fear, though the earth give way
and the mountains fall into the heart of the sea.

— *(Psalm 46:1,2)* —

Sooner or later you may find yourself in a hospital for the first time in your life. It can be a strange, frightening experience. The tests and procedures can be unpleasant. You miss your home, your family, even your own bed. You wonder what the tests and X rays will reveal, what surgery will be like if it becomes necessary, and how it will turn out. You are concerned about your family and wonder how they are coping. You have many questions and need many answers.

Where better to look for answers than in God's Word? He has much to say to those who may be hospitalized. Think for a moment of all the promises of God you know that seem specifically to speak to your present situation. Count up all the invitations you know in which he urges you to come to him in prayer. Consider all those reassuring "Fear nots" of God. You'll find at least one for every day of the year and every day you are in the hospital.

Do you hesitate to take this present need to him because you feel unworthy? Are you afraid that he may be angry over some sin you have committed? Then remember all that you've learned about Jesus. Remember what he did with your sins, which, though they were as scarlet, have become as white as snow through the blood of the Savior. The sin that is bothering you has already been punished in him who died as your substitute. Your debt is paid in full.

Be assured that God is *for* you in this illness, not against you, and all his wisdom and might are at work in your behalf. If you need even more assurance than that, you know that your pastor will gladly bring you the Lord's Supper in which your Savior gives you personally the very price he paid to redeem you, his body and blood.

You may still not understand how God can possibly forgive you, for his forgiveness is such a miracle of grace and mercy that it took the Holy Spirit to bring you to believe it. Even after receiving the Lord's Supper, you may not necessarily *feel* forgiven, but you will know that forgiveness is not a matter of feeling but of God's sure word and reliable promise. "This is my body," he says, "given for you" (Luke 22:19). "This is my blood . . . poured out for many for the forgiveness of sins," he continues (Matthew 26:28), and there is no more room for doubt.

You *are* God's redeemed child. He will be with you and see you safely through. He has a plan for your life that is as perfect as it is loving, and he is working out that plan in ways so high and wonderful that your mind cannot even grasp them. But you can trust him, for God has given you faith.

Take your misgivings to him in confident trust. Take your problems and fears to him, and leave them there for him to deal with. Imitate Daniel facing the lions in their den. Be like those three young men who faced a fiery furnace with the calm assurance: "The God we serve is able to save us" (Daniel 3:17). Know that he is a very present help in trouble, always coming to your rescue at the right time, never a moment too late.

May he give you a peaceful sleep this night as you entrust all things to his loving and mighty hands. He will not fail you.

— *Prayer* —

Lord, open our ears to hear your promises, our eyes to
see your loving mercy, and our hearts to believe your
Word, so that our fears will be replaced with an
unshakable trust and a calm and serene heart.
In Jesus' name we ask this. Amen.

10

HE SPEAKS TO YOU AS YOU ARE RECOVERING

Then Samuel took a stone and set it up between Mizpeh and Shen. He named it Ebenezer, saying, "Thus far has the LORD helped us."

— *(1 Samuel 7:12)* —

Many of us have gone through a serious illness and have known the intense relief of healing and recovery. Days of recovery are indeed pleasant times for us, but they can also be dangerous times—in some ways more dangerous than the illness itself. At first we are deeply thankful for our recovery, but how soon that feeling of gratitude can fade away! Then we are in danger of losing what God had hoped to accomplish through our illness and of missing out on blessings much greater than our healing. Illness can, in fact, be wasted!

When your illness grew worse and the situation seemed almost hopeless, you came to realize how dependent you are on God's help and mercy. Never in your life had you thought so seriously about your sins. Never had you prayed so fervently and often. You probably made all kinds of promises to God if only he would heal you. Never again would you doubt the power of prayer, the truth of his promises. Never again would you treat temptation lightly. That bad habit of yours was gone and forgotten. You truly intended to turn over a new leaf.

However deeply thankful you were at first, though, you found that as your health gradually returned, your illness did not seem as serious as it once had. God's healing may no longer have seemed so remarkable. Gradually you left all those eager promises behind. You prayed less often. You fought temptations less vigorously. You went your way much like the nine healed lepers who failed to return to Jesus with even a polite thank-you. Life was back to normal. You were well again.

Thank God if this is never a picture of your recovery. We do know it is a true picture of all too many people. For example, early in my ministry, I was called at midnight to the hospital bed of a man facing life-threatening surgery early in the morning. He was a powerful giant of a man, but he was thoroughly terrified. Now he did not feel so strong and secure. He needed someone more powerful than himself, but he had no religion and no idea where he should turn. It was a concerned nurse who asked me to come.

In the brief time I had with him, I led him through God's plan of salvation, I took him to the manger, to the cross, and to the empty tomb, inviting him to put his trust in that Savior who had died also for his sins. An amazing peace came over him. He was no longer the least bit afraid. In wonder I heard him say, "Why, he died for *me!*" He went into surgery with a peace he had never known before.

God mercifully spared his life and gave him a second chance. But although he tolerated my visits, once the danger was past, he felt he no longer needed the Lord he had just come to know. I never heard from him after he left the hospital. Think what he missed by failing to return to Jesus who was waiting to give him far greater blessings than physical healing. His illness was wasted.

Not so with Samuel. When the fierce Philistine warriors threatened to destroy Israel, the Lord sent such loud peals of thunder that the enemy fled in confusion. Samuel remembered the Lord's help and deliverance. He set up a monument to mark the occasion. It proclaimed, "Thus far has the LORD helped us."

In our times of recovery from illness, may we not waste the experience but return to the Lord with praise and thanksgiving, with a renewed trust, and with a deeper determination to avoid whatever might displease him. Let us seek a stronger faith and let us seek to lead a holier life by regular use of the means of grace. Having done so, we will discover the blessings God had in mind with our illness. Like Samuel's memorial stone, our whole lives will become monuments for people to see and read, "Thus far has the LORD helped us."

— *Prayer* —

Lord, with thankful hearts we remember how mercifully you have healed us. Grant that our recent illness may lead us to a deeper sense of gratitude and a greater desire to please you in all that we do. Amen.

11

HE SPEAKS TO YOU WHEN YOU ARE FEARFUL

"Fear not, for I have redeemed you; I have summoned you by name; you are mine."

— (Isaiah 43:1) —

One would hardly expect David, the writer of the 23rd psalm, to be afraid of anything. Even when he faced the prospect of death, he could say, "I will fear no evil" (verse 4). He reflected such fearlessness over and over in one psalm after the other. We hear it in Psalm 27, in 46, and in many others. We would expect such courage from the great psalmist, of course, but what about us ordinary, everyday Christians? Dare we hope for such serene peace and courage in the face of danger?

It may comfort us ordinary Christians to know that even the writer of such bold psalms had his moments of fear. He speaks of some of his fears, for example, in Psalm 34. But his fears did not get the best of him! He shows us how to deal with fear. He writes, "I sought the LORD, and . . . he delivered me from all my fears" (verse 4).

Here we see the secret of David's courage. He *sought* the Lord. This was the same sure remedy for fear used by Peter as he began to sink in the waves, by the disciples in the storm, and by Jonah in the belly of the great fish. David went boldly to the Lord, confident of his favor in the coming Savior. He went confidently, for his Lord was more powerful than any enemy or need or problem that confronted him. Had the Lord not said to Sarah when she doubted his promise that she would have a child in her old age, "Is anything too hard for the LORD?" (Genesis 18:14).

We have all learned how the Lord dealt in miraculous ways with the needs of his people both in the Old and New Testaments. When, in spite of better knowledge, fear still manages to sneak into our hearts in a crisis, it means that for the moment we have lost sight of the Lord's promises and of his mercy and wisdom and might. We are a little like Peter, who as he was walking on the water to Jesus took his eyes off Jesus and saw only the threatening waves. When he looked to the troubles and perils that confronted him, his faith failed. When, however, he looked to Jesus and reached out his hand to him for help, his troubles were over, replaced by a bolder faith. So it will be with us.

Our Lord has words for us in the Bible with which we can meet every fear and deal with every doubt. Over and over he tells us, "Fear not." This is not just a good friend speaking these marvelous words, one who wants to help but is unable. This is the Lord who understands our needs, who is full of compassion for us, who has the might to remove those needs and the wisdom to do it at just the right time and in the best way—the moment they have served his purpose for us.

In today's text, the Lord mentions reasons why God's children need not fear, " I have redeemed you; I have summoned you by name; you are mine." This assurance not only tells us not to fear but also *removes fear* and supplies the very boldness we need. He works in us such courage and peace of heart that often when the danger is past, we look back and wonder how we could have been afraid, armed as we were with such promises.

No, dear child of God, you need *never* fear—not anything. As David writes, "The LORD is the stronghold of my life—of whom shall I be afraid?" (Psalm 27:1). So this is your unfailing remedy for fear: simply keep your eyes on Jesus in every storm and crisis and know that he is at your side to deal with whatever comes into your life. So he has promised. So it will be.

— *Prayer* —

Dear Lord, how can I possibly fear when you, who knows all dangers, have told me over and over that I need not fear? May I joyfully sing in the face of any crisis: "In thine arms I rest me; Foes who would molest me Cannot reach me here. Though the earth be shaking, Every heart be quaking, Jesus calms my fear. Lightnings flash And thunders crash; Yet, though sin and hell assail me, Jesus will not fail me." Amen. (CW 349:2)

12

HE SPEAKS TO YOU
AS YOU FEAR AGING

"Even to your old age and gray hairs
I am he, I am he who will sustain you.
I have made you and I will carry you;
I will sustain you and I will rescue you."

— (Isaiah 46:4) —

Many people are dismayed when they recognize the first signs of aging in the mirror. They have seen in others what aging can bring with it. They are concerned about the weakening of their senses, the loss of independence, and the loneliness. A very old member I knew once remarked that old age is not for sissies. Another expressed the opinion that there is nothing very golden about the golden years.

Many fears about aging are simply not valid, and many of the problems associated with aging are really myths. It is simply not true that most old people are unhappy, helpless, grouchy, or senile; nor do most old people spend their last years in nursing homes.

Many do find it a golden time of life. They have matured as Christians and are ripe with a lifetime of experience with the Lord's loving care, his truth, his wisdom, and his power. They've learned that all of his promises are true, that he always answers prayer, that he never breaks his word. They have learned that he has a plan for them and that everything he does furthers that plan.

They've gained a wise sense of priorities over the years and know that many things in life that people frequently consider so important just don't count in the long run. The many hours they have spent under the guidance of the Holy Spirit have brought them to a clearer knowledge of themselves as sinners who need a Savior and to the heartfelt conviction that Jesus is that Savior. They know exactly where God is taking them and that through Jesus they will get there safely.

While shattering some of the myths of aging helps, it is much more comforting to be aware of the simple truth that God calls old age a special gift of love to those whom he cherishes. Now God never gives foolish, senseless, poorly chosen gifts—gifts that could harm us. He gives carefully and wisely, and that is true of his gift of old age as well.

We all know that aging may bring special burdens, but we are just as certain that those burdens always come with God's knowledge and permission and with a loving purpose. His purpose outweighs any suffering that age might bring. We also know that God himself walks side by side with us to help us bear what needs to be borne along the way, never allowing one ounce of misery more than we are able to bear.

Actually, he has prepared us through the years by giving us the faith and strength we need to meet whatever the years bring us. The promise that so sustained the apostle Paul through all his suffering, while he served the Lord, is also meant for us: "In all things God works for the good of those who love him" (Romans 8:28). We know that this promise does not suddenly run out when we reach a certain age!

Nor is old age all darkness. The prophet Zechariah tells us, "When evening comes, there will be light" (14:7). We look back over our lives, and now we are able to see God's love in events that seemed all wrong at the time. We discover how foolish we were to worry about things that God turned into blessings.

There will be days when our faith forgets and wavers for a moment, but the Holy Spirit will return us to a happy certainty. Around God's throne there is no darkness at all. There everything is bright as day. No mysteries perplex him. No problem in our lives is too complicated for him to solve.

At times we may wonder what the future may hold, but the Lord doesn't wonder. He knows every inch of the path that lies before us, and we can safely follow his guidance. Truly, "when evening comes, there will be light"—all the light we need to keep from losing our way.

If great old age is what God has chosen as his gift to you, consider it a mark of his tender love. Meet it confidently and serenely, eager to taste whatever wonders he still has in store for you before taking you to share those wonders which "no eye has seen, no ear has heard" (1 Corinthians 2:9). He has a plan for you, and that is really all you need to know, for his plan must have a happy ending—to be forever with the Lord.

— *Prayer* —

*"Throughout all their lifetime my people shall prove
My sovereign, eternal, unchangeable love, And then,
when gray hair shall their temples adorn, Like lambs
they shall still on my shoulders be borne."
Amen. (CW 416:5)*

HE SPEAKS TO YOU WHO TRUST IN THE LAMB

*"Look, the Lamb of God, who takes
away the sin of the world!"*

— *(John 1:29)* —

Years ago a Christmas card with a startling message arrived at my home. The card itself was just a simple line drawing of a lamb under which were printed five familiar words taken from a nursery rhyme: "Mary had a little lamb." At first glance that card and its message might have seemed an irreverent mockery of Christmas, but the more I thought about it, the more that message opened my eyes to the wonder of Bethlehem.

Listen carefully to the opening lines of that nursery rhyme, and you will notice how strikingly, though unintentionally, they help us to discover the joy that made the hearts of the Christmas shepherds pound with excitement. "Mary had a little lamb, its fleece was white as snow. And everywhere that Mary went, that lamb was sure to go."

Isn't that exactly what took place the night the angels sang for joy over our good fortune? For Mary *did* have a little lamb, the Lamb of God born to take away the sins of the world, the

Lamb "slain from the creation of the world" (Revelation 13:8), the Lamb "led . . . to the slaughter" (Acts 8:32) in our place, the Lamb in whose blood our robes were washed and made white (Revelation 7:14), even before the eyes of God, the Lamb who at his marriage supper would one day feed all "those whose names are written in the Lamb's book of life" (Revelation 21:27). The concept of Jesus as the Lamb is not new to us. We truly trust in the Lamb!

So Mary had a little Lamb born in the cold and filth and stench of a stable, the perfect Lamb, without spot or blemish, like the Passover lamb in Egypt. It took such a spotless Lamb to save us. Even this truth of Christ's purity and holiness unintentionally finds its way into that nursery rhyme when it says, "Its fleece was white as snow." Such a Lamb alone could turn God's anger away from us who deserved it. The Lamb took it all upon himself. He became what we were, that we might become what he is—holy, righteous, beloved sons and daughters of God.

We could pursue the thought of that nursery rhyme a line further: "And everywhere that Mary went, that lamb was sure to go." For Mary's Lamb is the omnipresent Son of God, not confined to her arms or to that stable or even to Palestine or this planet, for he was and is everywhere present at all times. That Lamb *did* follow Mary all her life, protecting her from the rage of Herod and the anger of the enemies at the cross, giving her peace of heart and mind. Even at the cross, the Lamb provided for Mary by saying to John, "Here is your mother" (John 19:27).

Marvel with all the saints at this wonder: that same Lamb of God is with *you* wherever you go. He is in complete, loving control of your life. "Surely," he promises, "I am with you always" (Matthew 28:20). "Never will I leave you; never will I forsake you" (Hebrew 13:5).

It is very likely not even close to Christmas as you read this page, but that is good. It reminds you that you have an exciting message of Christmas to cheer your heart every day of the year. We need that reminder.

What a wondrous thought! God's Son has been born to assure you of a year-round white Christmas and a "white" life in God's sight. That Lamb became stained with our sins so that we might take refuge in Isaiah's words: "Though your sins are like scarlet, they shall be as white as snow; though they are red as crimson, they shall be like wool" (Isaiah 1:18).

How exciting it will be one day to join the mass choir of angels singing around the throne of the Lamb: "Worthy is the Lamb, who was slain, to receive power and wealth and wisdom and strength and honor and glory and praise! . . . To him who sits on the throne and to the Lamb be praise and honor and glory and power, for ever and ever!" (Revelation 5:12,13).

Truly, "Mary had a little Lamb!" Let's join to thank God with all his saints!

— *Prayer* —

**Heavenly Father, Mary had the Lamb in whom
she trusted for her salvation, the Lamb she could
call her Lord and Redeemer. You have given us that
Lamb too by faith. May Jesus truly be our comfort
and strength and ever bring peace to our hearts.
In his name we ask it. Amen.**

14

HE SPEAKS TO YOU WHEN YOU GRIEVE

"You will grieve, but your grief will turn to joy."

— *(John 16:20)* —

Jesus was speaking to his disciples who were about to experience incredible grief. He was about to be taken from them and nailed to a cross, and they would lose not only their best friend and sure protector but also the one they'd come to know as their Savior and Lord. Their hopes were about to be buried with him in a tomb.

Not one of us has gone through grief exactly like that, but we have all experienced the sadness of standing at the grave of a very important and precious person—someone whom we loved dearly. What do these words, spoken by Jesus to his desperate disciples, say to us? How can they help heal our wounds?

Let's listen carefully. Notice that Jesus told his disciples about the grief that was to come to them before it actually occurred. What was about to happen was not some unexpected tragedy that caught Jesus unaware. He was well aware of what lay ahead for him on Good Friday and could easily have avoided those fateful events. He simply could have avoided Jerusalem at that time, or for that matter, he could have crushed his enemies as easily as he brought them to the ground in Gethsemane.

Actually, his enemies were never in control of events. Rather, his dying was part of God's plan, conceived together with his Son already in eternity. Jesus permitted these awful things to happen, not because he was helpless to ward them off but because they were involved in the only plan that could save sinners.

His advance announcement of his dying thus already contained comfort for the disciples, but Jesus said much more! "Your grief will turn to joy." He was not merely promising that time would eventually heal their wounds and help them to forget how sad they had been on Good Friday. Listen carefully. Their grief would *turn to* joy.

Once they understood what the death of Jesus meant for them, their very reason for grief and sorrow on Good Friday would become the reason for their greatest comfort. It would become the basis of all their hopes, and the theme of every sermon they would preach. By his death they lived! It was actually a reason to celebrate—a reason to thank God. It was the message they would bring to a dying world: "We preach Christ crucified" (1 Corinthians 1:23).

Let's apply the words of Jesus to the grief we feel as we stand beside an open grave. This death of a loved one did not just happen by accident or chance either. It didn't take place without Christ's knowledge or permission. It was not a surprise victory of Satan or a failure of our Savior's plans for one whom he loved more than we did or ever could.

He forewarned us, as he did the disciples, that we would know such sadness. He knew exactly when it would come, and, yes, he could have turned it aside. After all, he is the Lord, mightier than any heart attack or virus. He permitted it because it was the best way to fulfill his plan to receive our loved one safely to heaven. And just as he promised the disciples that one day they would understand and praise God, so we will arrive at that point. We will, in fact, praise God for the very event that made us so sad at the time.

It is not easy to lose a loved one. We recall how Jesus wept at the death of his friend Lazarus. Even today it is no light matter to him when one of his dear children dies. He does not enjoy seeing us grieve, because he loves us. So he hastens to promise that we shall one day understand, and then our "grief will turn to joy."

His Word tells us, "Precious in the sight of the LORD is the death of his saints" (Psalm 116:15). They've reached their real home and are already experiencing a kind of peace and joy and wonder that we cannot even imagine. They are out of reach of every disappointment and pain, beyond all danger of losing their inheritance as the sons and daughters of God.

Let this be your deep comfort in every sorrow and sadness: "Your grief will turn to joy."

— *Prayer* —

Lord, we sometimes wallow in self-pity
and sorrow. Help us remember that you are
even now acting in a love that is complete
and in a wisdom that is absolute. Amen.

15

HE SPEAKS TO YOU DURING SLEEPLESS NIGHTS

My eyes stay open through the watches of the night,
that I may meditate on your promises.

— *(Psalm 119:148)* —

Sleep is one of those blessings of God we too often take for granted. How we miss it, however, when we go without it night after night. Those sleepless nights affect us physically, mentally, and emotionally, making the days seem endless and making our dispositions sour and our labors a struggle. We can understand how Job felt when he spoke of tossing and turning back and forth until dawn.

Why does the Lord permit us to lie awake for nights on end if he loves us as much as he says? Doesn't he himself tell us that "he grants sleep to those he loves" (Psalm 127:2)? Does sleeplessness therefore suggest that he no longer loves us?

Experts give endless advice on the subject, but their advice does not seem to work for us. Friends advise us to count sheep, but that too fails. What does help? Would it not help to look to the Shepherd instead of counting his sheep? Even

45

our Shepherd withdrew from the crowds and went off by himself to meditate.

Haven't we found how difficult it is for us to concentrate on God's Word when we are distracted by all kinds of noisy, hectic activity? We sometimes wish that we could turn off all the machines and radios and TVs for just a little while and have some completely quiet, uncluttered hours in which to meditate, undisturbed and undistracted, on God's Word.

We do have such a time. Perhaps we do not always recognize what a precious time it can be, so we fail to make use of it. Can there be a quieter, less interrupted time than the quiet hours of the night to focus all our attention on him who loves us and gave himself for us and on his promises that cover every situation in our lives?

What better time could there be to let God speak to us about his loving purposes for us—if not from the pages of that book on our nightstand, than from the pages of mind and memory that years ago stored up many Bible passages and hymn verses? We can draw on them again and meditate upon them in the quiet of the night. More and more these treasures will come back to us, and night after night the Holy Spirit will use those gems to lead us deeper and deeper into God's truth.

You may decide, as I have, that those hours spent at memory work in school may have been the most lasting and vital part of our schooling. Those memorized words, almost forgotten, but now remembered again, make sleepless hours not only endurable but even enriching, rewarding, and exciting. That should not surprise us, for God is showing the same love when he withholds a precious gift like sleep as when he gives it.

No, our minds have not become too old and worn to recall those hymns and Bible verses and catechism truths. Other muscles need to be used to remain effective. So it is with our minds. I recall a man in his eighties who scarcely had an eighth-grade education and had great difficulty reading. Yet he found peace of heart by memorizing in German all the many stanzas of the prolific hymn writer Paul Gerhardt.

Try this yourself, perhaps begin by memorizing the Bible verses at the beginning of the devotions in this book. Then, when God in his wisdom chooses to withhold sleep, draw on such passages, listening for the truth with which God would enrich your life and draw you closer to him. Don't fret about those hours. Don't waste those sleepless nights. Use them to be drawn closer to the Lord. Use them to store up strength for the hectic hours of the morrow.

You can trust God to know what you need. He knows when sleepless nights will serve you better even than quiet slumber. Don't count sheep. Look to the Good Shepherd. Listen for his voice, and let him guide, comfort, and enlighten you. And pray for sleep-filled nights to return when the Lord himself chooses.

— *Prayer* —

Lord, how frustrated we become when
night after night we wait sleepless for the dawn.
Help us to see your loving hand even then and
to use those hours in getting to know you
and your truths even better. Amen.

16

HE SPEAKS TO YOU AS YOU STAND BESIDE A SICKBED

Now a man named Lazarus was sick. He was from Bethany, the village of Mary and her sister Martha. So the sisters sent word to Jesus, "Lord, the one you love is sick."

— *(John 11:1,3)* —

Most of us have, at one time or another, sat with deep concern at the sickbed of a loved member of the family. Maybe we watched anxiously as the situation grew worse day by day. What can God say to us to quiet our misgivings and concerns in such a difficult time?

Today he takes us to a home in ancient Bethany. Two sisters named Mary and Martha are going through this situation with their seriously ill brother, Lazarus. We learn a valuable lesson from the manner in which they dealt with this crisis.

Notice first that these people were not strangers to Jesus. They were among his very dearest friends. The gospel account repeatedly stresses that Jesus loved these people. He was not angry with them, nor was he punishing them. This realization should quiet any misgivings we might sometimes have, because we are reminded that illness and trouble do come to those who love the Lord, and who are deeply loved by him. Illness is not to be taken as a sign that we have been rejected by the Lord or as evidence that he does not love us.

Next we notice how these friends of Jesus immediately reacted. "The sisters sent word to Jesus." And what did they tell him? Did they tell him that he was not treating his friends very well? Did they presume to tell him how he should help?

No! They simply brought their need to him. They were confident that he would provide the best answer. What he decided would be good enough for them. Later in the account, we see that trust shining through again. Even when Jesus, for reasons of his own, permitted Lazarus to die, they continued to trust in him. We hear Martha say: "Lord, . . . if you had been here, my brother would not have died. But I know that even now God will give you whatever you ask" (John 11:21,22).

We want to learn one more lesson from the sickbed prayer of these sisters. They had shown much kindness to Jesus when he was a guest in their home. Yet, notice that they do not base their claim for help on the love that they had shown him—as if he owed them this.

Their claim was based on a much surer hope—*his* love. "The one you love is sick" was their appeal. Their love was human and might have wavered, but his love for them would not. That love was a fact they could rely on. It was reflected in his reaction to the illness of Lazarus. John writes, "He was deeply moved in spirit and troubled" (John 11:33). Then, in the shortest verse in the Bible, John reports that "Jesus wept" (John 11:35). Such is the loving concern of our friend Jesus in our illnesses and in those of our loved ones. We see how deeply he cares. These were simple, uneducated people, but how wise they were and how much we can learn from them as we ourselves go through illness with a family member! They went to Jesus. They trusted his decision. They depended on his love for them. They continued to trust him, even when their prayer seemed to be unheeded.

We want to keep this beautiful account in our hearts for the day when the Lord may decide to permit us to sit at the bedside of a loved one who is gravely ill. Then we will accept our situation as a mark of his love, not as a mark of his anger. We will go at once to Jesus. We will trust his judgment. We will rely totally on his proven love for us, not on what we think he may owe us. We will not presume to tell him how to help, but we will simply lay the need at his feet, leaving the issue to his wisdom and love. "Lord, the one you love is sick." Having done this, we can wait in serene peace for his answer—for the help he has promised. He will never fail us.

— *Prayer* —

**Make us wise, Lord, like Mary and
Martha. Help us direct our needs at once to Jesus,
not telling him when and how to help, not basing our
plea on our love for him or what we have done for
him, but simply bringing this illness to him and
relying on his wisdom to know what is best.
We ask this in Jesus' name. Amen.**

17

HE SPEAKS TO YOU WHEN YOU FEEL FORSAKEN

But Zion said, "The LORD has
forsaken me, the Lord has forgotten me."
"Can a mother forget the baby at her breast
and have no compassion on the child she has borne?
Though she may forget, I will not forget you."

— (Isaiah 49:14,15) —

Aging makes the feeling of being forsaken almost inevitable. Many of our best friends are no longer around or are unable to visit us. Our children have moved out of the house—often so far away that we get to see them only rarely. Our daily contacts at the workplace are history. Little wonder that a pastor frequently hears these complaints from the elderly: "No one comes to see me. Nobody cares what is happening to me or how I am doing. I'm alone and forsaken. The days seem so long and empty."

For friends to forget about us is bad enough. But what if the Lord himself has forsaken us? What if he is too busy with the big things of the world, the rise and fall of nations or the guidance of the stars, to even be aware of little, sinful, unworthy me? What if I am lost in the huge mass of billions of people? How can he possibly even notice my small voice whispering a prayer when billions of prayers must rise to his throne every hour?

To be forsaken by the Lord would be a disaster, indeed. So what can we do about that terrible sinking feeling that comes upon us when we call upon him for help and there seems to be no relief? Has the Lord become sick and tired of us because we have forsaken him, ignored him, or even defied his will? Has he become so weary of us that he has decided to leave us on our own? What can he possibly say to us today to assure us that he has not forsaken us and will never do so?

The simple answer to this concern is that God has time and again promised never to leave us or forsake us. One such promise would have been sufficient, but we possess so many. And if we feel unworthy of such precious promises, we need only look to Jesus on the cross. There our Savior was actually forsaken by his Father under the burden of our sins. He endured being forsaken for us. He took away all reason for God to forsake us. Therefore, we need never fear, even in times of trouble, that God has forsaken us. Because of Good Friday, he says to us, "I know the plans I have for you, . . . plans to prosper you and not to harm you, plans to give you hope and a future" (Jeremiah 29:11).

We love also the comforting assurance God gives us through the prophet Isaiah: "Can a mother forget the baby at her breast and have no compassion on the child she has borne? Though she may forget, I will not forget you."

With what love and compassion a mother watches over her child! Yet we hear, more and more, of mothers who forsake their children. But that cannot possibly happen with God. He never forgets the children he purchased to be his own at such tremendous cost. They may forget him for a long time, but he always remains faithful and uses every possible means to bring them back.

Sometimes he finds it necessary to use a long illness to remind them of their sin, their need of forgiveness, and their need for him. In all these experiences, he has not forsaken them but is working out his purposes for them. He promises, "Though she may forget, I will not forget you."

When it seems that no one cares about you, know assuredly that God will never cease to care. He who is closer to you even than your own mother could be. Forsaken by him? Never!

The soul that on Jesus hath leaned for repose
I will not, I will not, desert to his foes;
That soul, though all hell should endeavor to shake,
I'll never, no never, no never, forsake! (TLH 427:7)

— *Prayer* —

Dear Lord, how sad I am over my lack of faith.
How can I possibly feel forsaken when you
have promised to always be with me? Help me
cling to your promise never to forsake me.
"Be near me, Lord Jesus; I ask you to stay
Close by me forever and love me,
I pray." Amen. (CW 68:3)

18

HE SPEAKS TO YOU WHEN YOU ARE PROSPERING

When you eat and are satisfied, be careful that you do not forget the LORD, who brought you out of Egypt, out of the land of slavery.

— *(Deuteronomy 6:11,12)* —

Most of us experience times when things are going quite well. Our families are in good health, we're prospering at our professions, no major problems threaten us. These are good times, and we would like them to continue. But if we are not careful, such good times may become bad times, even dangerous times. It has been said that no nation has ever withstood prosperity very long, and that is often true of individuals as well.

Several things seem to happen to people when they are prospering. They become proud and self-sufficient, and they no longer feel a real need for God in their lives. They forget the debt of gratitude they owe him for their prosperity and their dependence on him for everything they have. Gradually they may even drift away from God. The Lord and his Word no longer seem so important, and they thanklessly go their way. They spend less time in prayer. They are seen less often at worship.

That is why we say that prosperous times may become dangerous times. That is why God repeatedly warns us to be careful in connection with gratitude.

In today's Bible passage, he says to us, "When you eat and are satisfied, be careful that you do not forget the LORD." He considers this warning important enough to repeat it two chapters later, "Be careful that you do not forget the LORD. . . . Otherwise, when you eat and are satisfied, when you build fine houses and settle down, and when your herds and flocks grow large and your silver and gold increase and all you have is multiplied, then your heart will become proud and you will forget the LORD your God" (Deuteronomy 8:11-14).

The words of Jesus would also apply: "What good is it for a man to gain the whole world, yet forfeit his soul? Or what can a man give in exchange for his soul?" (Mark 8:36,37).

Surely we want to be thankful and happy when we are prospering, recognizing that the gracious hand of God is behind this bounty. As we turn to God with thankful hearts, we find even greater blessings than material gain, blessings for our souls. Such blessings were lost, for example, by the nine healed lepers who went their way without thanking Jesus for what he had done for them. How eternally rich Jesus could have made them! But they remained poor toward God. So may our prosperous times direct us to God in thankful praise. They dare not cause us to drift from him as though we no longer need him.

And what if our time of prosperity ends? When God chooses to withhold prosperity, he is not loving us one bit less. He knows that there are times and seasons when we need less more than we need plenty. We need to learn that there is a lot more to life than buying and selling at a profit. We need to know that, even with all of our education and knowledge, we are still completely dependent on God for everything. We must learn to put first things first and seek first the kingdom of God and his righteousness, knowing that, as we do this, God will "throw in" all the lesser things we need for good measure.

It is not God-pleasing when we bemoan the "bad" times or fail to learn the lesson God would teach us through them. But neither does he want us to waste the prosperous times, for they give us reason to thank and praise God more fervently, to serve him more eagerly, and to trust him more surely.

— *Prayer* —

God of all goodness, help us never
to forget the source of all blessings, knowing
that "every good and perfect gift is from above,
coming down from the Father of the heavenly
lights" (James 1:17). We thank you for the
abundance of your blessings. May we never,
because of all your blessings, forget
our need for you. Amen.

HE SPEAKS TO YOU AS YOU FACE RETIREMENT

[The righteous] will still bear fruit in old age,
they will stay fresh and green, proclaiming,
"The LORD is upright."

— *(Psalm 92:14,15)* —

The word *retirement* was hardly in the vocabulary of our parents and grandparents. They worked until they could not work any more. Today many people leave the workplace while they are still in their sixties.

What kind of experience is retirement for them? Many find it a pleasant, unhurried, and relaxed time. It is an escape from the pressures of work and the hectic schedules that left little time for family or for activities like traveling, reading, or fishing. It seems safe to say that most people, but certainly not all, can't wait to retire.

Actually, retirement is a mixed bag. As the date draws nearer, people long for retirement and dread it at the same time. Some are concerned about the loss of income and of independence. Some worry about becoming a burden to their children or even to society. They suspect they will feel totally useless and be thought of as "over the hill." They expect that they will no longer be valued as persons. Few people, if any, will come to them for advice. Their experiences will no longer be valued. Will their lives be without purpose?

God, as always, has answers for such misgivings as well as for the burdens that retirement may bring. A simple answer to our misgivings is the truth that old age is a special gift of God to his children, and his gifts are always perfect, just right for us. He says to us, "With long life will I satisfy him and show him my salvation" (Psalm 91:16). Again, "However many years a man may live, let him enjoy them all" (Ecclesiastes 11:8). Retirement would hardly be a real blessing if it meant that suddenly we have no way to serve God and live unto him.

In our text the psalmist suggests that God's children will indeed bring forth fruit in their old age. They will produce fruits and continue to stay green and vital. We call them mature, and the word *mature* does not suggest decay or dying, but ripeness, fulfillment, perfection. It brings to mind the mature fruit on a tree. A better term for the elderly then might be mature citizens, not senior citizens.

Retirement years need not be useless years. They can be rich and full—complete and satisfying. Our purpose in life has not limped to an end. Actually, it has been enhanced in many ways. Our many years of experience with God's love, truth, and grace have not only strengthened us for service, they are experiences we can draw on to share with others and enrich their lives. We have tasted God's love, patience, guidance, and protection, and we've gained a wiser sense of values and know what really counts in life. We can pass that knowledge on to others.

In retirement we have more time to serve, to witness, and to pray. Perhaps, above all, we have learned how to pray for others. We've often heard some ill or elderly Christian say rather plaintively and sadly, "Well, at least I can still pray," as though that were some trivial thing! Trivial? It is one of the greatest things we can do for others—bringing their needs to the throne of God.

We can and will pray for our church and its pastors and for the straying and the sick. We can pray that God's Word will reach the hearts of the unchurched or the hardened. We can pray for the spiritual well-being of our own families. And when almost too weak to gather our thoughts for praying, we can use the Lord's Prayer, which Luther compared to a big basket in which we carry all our needs to God—they are all covered by that prayer!

If you fear that in retirement you will be useless, lay that fear to rest. God will give you opportunity and strength to serve him. He can provide the time and skills to do what you have always wanted to do but for which you had little time.

You can surely "bear fruit in old age." Your life can still make a real difference. Perhaps you will even decide that life begins not at forty but at retirement!

— *Prayer* —

Lord, the paths ahead seem much like unknown
highways. Please be there beside us, and help
us look forward expectantly and confidently.
Bless our retirement years, and guide us
in living them to your praise. Amen.

20

HE SPEAKS TO YOU
ABOUT A POWERFUL ALLY

Moses answered the people, "Do not be afraid.
Stand firm and you will see the deliverance
the LORD will bring you today. The Egyptians
you see today you will never see again. The LORD
will fight for you; you need only to be still."

— *(Exodus 14:13,14)* —

How often we discover how weak and defenseless we are and how desperately we need a powerful ally! Today, God uses Moses to lead us to just such a powerful ally, one who can handle any enemy and has promised to fight for us.

Through the wonders of the ten plagues, God had enabled Moses to lead Israel out of Egypt's slavery. Before long, however, things looked so dark for God's people once again that they actually wished that they were back in the misery from which they had just been delivered.

Though the plagues had exposed the "nothingness" of the gods in which Pharaoh and his people trusted, Pharaoh changed his mind again about allowing the Israelites to depart. He sent his powerful forces—his riders and his chariots—to drag God's people back. There seemed to be no escape for Israel, no hope at all. The Red Sea lay ahead of them and the Egyptian army was coming up fast behind them. The masses of Israel quickly forgot God's wonders and despaired, but Moses remembered. He knew that God would not forsake his people.

There was, as always, one place to turn for help, and that was to the God of their salvation. The odds against victory were overwhelming, until one remembered the ally who was on their side. "The LORD will fight for you," Moses told the people. God did fight for them in a manner that should have removed any future temptation for the Israelites to despair or to rely on their own might. He divided the waters of the Red Sea, and his chosen ones walked through on dry ground. When the waters came together again, the pursuing horses and chariots of the Egyptians perished. Small wonder that God's people were delivered! The Lord himself was fighting for them. He was their all-powerful ally.

How secure the experience of those Israelites ought to make us feel! The same mighty Lord fights for us, his chosen people. As we go forth to do battle against any enemy or problem, we bear on the front of our shields Paul's fear-banishing words: "If God is for us, who can be against us?" (Romans 8:31).

And God is for us, as he so vividly demonstrated when he spared not his own Son but delivered him up for us all. He did this for us while we were yet his enemies, living in active rebellion against him, and before we had lifted one finger to serve him or had raised one song of praise to his throne. Surely we know that he is fighting for us now that we are cleansed of all sin by the blood of his Son, now that we are his saints, his redeemed ones, his friends, his children.

"Fear not," he assures us, "for I have redeemed you; I have summoned you by name; you are mine. When you pass through the waters, I will be with you; and when you pass through the rivers, they will not sweep over you. When you walk through the fire, you will not be burned. . . . For I am the LORD, your God" (Isaiah 43:1-3).

We don't expect to face walls of water, as the Israelites or the pursuing army did, or the flames of a fiery furnace, as did those three young men in Babylon. Our deliverance may not be as dramatic, but deliver us he will. Those terror-stricken Israelites, as well as those three calm young men, are symbols of the worst of dangers that may threaten our lives, symbols of the deliverance we can expect from him who promises to fight for us and does so.

He is our refuge and strength as he was for the psalmist who could therefore say, "We will not fear, though the earth give way and the mountains fall into the heart of the sea" (Psalm 46:2). Take with you into battle faith's sure answer to the question, "Is anything too hard for the LORD?" (Genesis 18:14), and remember the confident words of Moses to a people in danger: "The LORD will fight for you." That's good enough for me. How about you?

— *Prayer* —

"If God himself be for me, I may a host defy; For when I pray, before me My foes, confounded, fly. If Christ, my head and master, Befriend me from above, What foe or what disaster Can drive me from his love?" Amen. (CW 419:1)

21

HE SPEAKS TO YOU WHEN YOU ARE DISCOURAGED

Why are you downcast, O my soul?
Why so disturbed within me?
Put your hope in God, for I will yet
praise him, my Savior and my God.

— (Psalm 42:5,6) —

Here you see a side of the psalmist that may surprise you. This great hero of faith was distressed and troubled! We wonder how a man of such soaring faith could ever have had one moment of depression.

It quickly occurs to us that the psalmist was not the only one ever to have such feelings of discouragement. Luther at one point was so bothered by the slow progress the Reformation was making that he became extremely downcast. Knowing he was in such a terrible mood, his wife, Katie, came into his study wearing the black of mourning. He took one look at her and asked who had died. She replied, "Why, judging from the way you're acting, I assumed God is dead!" He quickly caught on and went back to work with a new attitude.

We have all shared such moments of discouragement. Perhaps we have even wondered at times whether we actually were Christians. Have we come to believe that God's children should never be discouraged? It should help us to remember that such depressing moments happened to David, to Luther, and surely to many, if not most, of the heroes of faith. God knows how human we are and has a message for us. He evidently considered this message very important, for we find it repeated three times on one page in the Bible.

First, we note that the psalmist who wrote these words had not stopped being a believer. The text makes that clear. This already is of comfort to us when we find ourselves discouraged. We need not despair.

We note also the psalmist's realization that he had no right to feel as he did. He was so unhappy with himself that he took himself to task, "Why are you downcast, O my soul?" It is as though he were rebuking himself: "What right have you to feel discouraged? When has God ever let you down?"

This is also how those frightened disciples of Jesus should have felt when, only hours after witnessing a mighty miracle of Jesus, they despaired in a storm at sea, even with the Lord right there in the ship with them. Do you recall his words? "You of little faith, why are you so afraid?" (Matthew 8:26). Had the ship gone straight to the bottom of the sea, they still would have had no reason to despair with the Lord of wonders with them. How could they have forgotten so soon?

David remembered his faith. "Put your hope in God, for I will yet praise him, my Savior and my God." God had promised to keep him safe at all times and to prosper his work. God had a plan for his life and work, and that was all

64

he needed to know. Help would arrive at just the right time and in the right way. David himself called God "an ever-present help in trouble" (Psalm 46:1), in other words, help that always comes in time.

God has spoken what we need to know and apply in our hours of discouragement. At times, while we *hear* the words of God, we somehow *do not get their message*.

We want to remember, to our great comfort, that he, who at our baptisms planted faith in our hearts, is able to scatter those clouds of doubt that sometimes hang over us. Then we really will see clearly again that around God's throne there is no darkness at all. There everything is bright as day; no mysteries perplex him, no problems are too hard for him to solve.

God will come to your aid also in this present need, and soon you will bask again in the warm sunshine of his love. David expected that. He said, "I will yet praise him, my Savior and my God." In the next verse, he explains, "I will remember you" (Psalm 42:6).

May you remember him too, and in all your needs, trust him for the help that is sure to come.

— *Prayer* —

Dear Father, forgive me for my disturbing moments of doubt and discouragement. Help me remember you and your promises and be content to wait for the relief that you will surely send. Amen.

22

HE SPEAKS TO YOU WHEN YOU ARE EMBITTERED

"You intended to harm me, but
God intended it for good."

— *(Genesis 50:20)* —

In envy Joseph's brothers had sold him to a caravan of traders who carted him off to Egypt to be sold as a slave. How ironically things turned out for him. As his story unfolds, we see striking evidence of the providence of God and the way he works things out to the advantage of his children. Joseph prospered in a most mysterious way. Joseph, a onetime slave and prisoner, was elevated to a position of authority second only to Pharaoh. Joseph became God's agent for keeping his chosen nation alive during a terrible famine, a famine that forced Jacob's family to come to Egypt seeking food.

Now we see Joseph's brothers before him. They had done him great harm. He could so easily have been embittered toward them. Now he has the opportunity to take his revenge. But—can you believe it?—listen to his words: "You intended to harm me, but God intended it for good."

Joseph's words not only show forgiving love toward his brothers, but they also express an understanding of God's control and care over his life. Joseph saw that God was, in fact, using his brothers' hostile plans to carry out his purposes of love, not only for Joseph and his people but for us and all Christians to the end of time. By preserving the family of Jacob from famine and extinction, God kept alive his promise of a Savior who was to come from this people.

We recognize this providence of God, set forth on so many pages of Scripture, sometimes in most dramatic ways. Hundreds of years after this event, for example, we see God's hand in the lives of Daniel and his three young friends, slaves in the land of Babylon. We see God's purposes at work in the case of a woman named Esther, whom he, in the interest of his people, elevated to the position of queen. We watch as God, in a most striking manner, used a heathen ruler, Caesar Augustus, to set in motion his whole kingdom with a census. That census made it possible for God's Son to be born in tiny Bethlehem as foretold. Later God would also use Pontius Pilate and his soldiers as the instruments of his plan of salvation.

"God intended it for good" was the way Joseph put it. These stories of famous people who have been used by God are intertwined with the lives and histories of every last ordinary child of God. All have been touched and guided by his providence. All have been protected and drawn to him in strange and wonderful ways. We are reminded of the words of the prophet Jeremiah: "I have loved you with an everlasting love; I have drawn you with loving-kindness" (31:3).

There are occasions when we too are inclined to become bitter. Everything seems to have gone against us. Our plans have failed. We've been disappointed in our hopes. At such times, we want to keep in mind the words of Joseph to his malicious brothers: "God intended it for good." When evil, or what seems like evil, comes our way, we want to have that same confidence. Whatever men may do to us or whatever obstacles life may throw in our paths, this fact remains true: "God intended it for good."

What security this gives us! It helps us overcome feelings of revenge and forgive those who wrong us. God will let no evil overcome us or enemies harm us. Remember, he loves us. If vengeance is called for, we leave that in the hands of God.

Is your life full of bitterness today? Has someone wronged you time and again? Leave it in God's hands. He will turn around their bad intentions. "Pray for those who persecute you" (Matthew 5:44), as Jesus urges you to do, and look to the example of him who when he was cursed, cursed not again. Reflect the forgiving spirit of Joseph toward his brothers, because that is how Jesus treats you. This is one way to say thank you to God for his mercy toward you.

— *Prayer* —

Help us accept the fact that there will always
be people who for some reason will misuse and
mistreat us, as Joseph's brothers did to him. Let us
trust in your promises to keep us in your care.
Thank you, Lord, for your promise to make
all things work together for our good. Amen.

23

HE SPEAKS TO YOU
ABOUT LOW SELF-ESTEEM

Dear friends, now we are children of God,
and what we will be has not yet been made known.

— (1 John 3:2) —

It is almost bound to happen that aging brings with it a sense of low self-worth, of low self-esteem. Even if in our earlier years we were respected for certain accomplishments and looked up to for various achievements, all that seems to be easily forgotten. We may begin to feel very much like a nobody—that we are just a bother to people or that we just take up space. It seems as though it would make little difference if we were no longer around.

Are we still worth anything? The biochemist has one answer. He weighs the chemicals in a human body and decides that we are worth only a few dollars. That, of course, says nothing about our value to our loved ones. More important, it says nothing about the value God has placed on us. Through the many gracious acts by which he has made us his own, he has established our worth to him.

Back in eternity, he knew us and chose us to be his own. He wanted us in his family and in heaven. He knew that we would be born lost in sin, but he planned a most costly way to make us his people again, in spite of our condition. As the most lavish display of his loving concern for us, he sent his beloved Son to be born in a stable to a lowly virgin and to live in poverty. He would say of himself, "Foxes have holes and birds of the air have nests, but the Son of Man has no place to lay his head" (Matthew 8:20). He endured abuse, shame, and agony to redeem us, dying a death so awful that it was deemed unfit for all but the worst criminals. That was the price God placed on us, the cost he gladly paid to redeem us unto himself.

That cost of our redemption totally dwarfs the cost of any price ever paid for anything else in this world. Imagine then what value we have in the sight of God. Just think for a moment of the titles he has given us. John mentions one, "Dear friends, now we are children of God." At other times, God calls us saints, the redeemed, the children of light, the apple of his eye, the heirs of God, the members of his kingdom and family, his beloved, his friends. God calls you and me that!

So do you consider yourself worthless and of no consequence? If the world's most powerful ruler adopted you into his family, would you feel worthless then? But here, it is God who has done just that!

Surely we will always want to remember that of ourselves we are nothing and have nothing to bring to God as payment for even one tiny sin. Such humility will move us to bring our empty cups to him to be filled with his righteousness, his wisdom, his worth, and his strength. But though we have no worth of our own, we do have value to God, who paid such an awesome price for us. We are his very own. We possess heaven as our inheritance.

When your spirit is broken and you are overcome with a feeling of worthlessness, then remember who you became at your baptism. Remember who is bothering to lead you safely through this life. Remember who is awaiting you with open arms to welcome you home. You do have worth—the worth that is yours in the One who redeemed you with his lifeblood as the price.

— *Prayer* —

Lord, when we consider our sinfulness
and unworthiness, we wonder how you can
have any use for us. Remind us then of the cross
and what it has made of us and of the wonders
your Holy Spirit has worked in us. May we—
as your very own children, saints, and
friends—glory in the cross of Jesus. Amen.

24

HE SPEAKS TO YOU AS YOU LONG FOR GOD'S HOUSE

As the deer pants for streams of water, so my soul pants for you, O God. My soul thirsts for God, for the living God. When can I go and meet with God? These things I remember as I pour out my soul: how I used to go with the multitude, leading the procession to the house of God, with shouts of joy and thanksgiving among the festive throng.

— *(Psalm 42:1,2,4)* —

When you spent a week with relatives as a child, you probably tasted the painful bitterness of being homesick. They probably could not have been kinder to you, but you missed your home and family so much that you were almost physically ill, barely able to swallow food. You were homesick, and the only remedy for this was to get back home again.

Another kind of homesickness may be even more painful, and it strikes us more severely as we grow old. It is the longing for God's house that we feel after a long absence, made necessary, perhaps, by illness.

Going to church is a privilege we have taken for granted throughout the years, as if that special joy of worship and fellowship and that sweet comfort of hearing God's Word from the pulpit would always be ours. But that is all in the past for some of us, at least for now. We may listen to the radio service of one or more of our churches in the area. We may even get to see our congregation's service on television, but it is not the same as being there. We begin to understand how the psalmist felt: "I love the house where you live, O LORD, the place where your glory dwells" (Psalm 26:8). Life isn't the same; we are homesick for God's house.

The psalmist seems to be speaking of that kind of home-sickness in Psalm 42, in which he talks of his thirsting for God, his longing to "go and meet with God." With longing, he remembers what a joy that used to be for him and writes, "I used to go with the multitude, leading the procession to the house of God, with shouts of joy and thanksgiving."

The psalmist missed the house of God. He was homesick for it and wanted to be there once again. He would have appreciated just how you feel when, for some reason or other, you are kept from attending your church. You miss the warm fellowship, the familiar hymns, and the beauty of your church. You especially long to hear again from your pulpit the comforting Word of God, which in another psalm is compared to honey (Psalm 119:103).

Of course we join with you in praying that you will once again experience this joy, perhaps even on a regular basis. God can manage that. But if he decides otherwise, remember what you have *not* lost. David was surrounded by heathen who mocked his religion, his trust in God, and his deep desire to seek refuge in God's house with God's people. Unlike

73

David, you very likely have not lost the support and love of faithful Christian friends who visit you and share their faith with you.

Your pastor comes and makes your home his pulpit. He brings you the same message you would have heard in church and the same Lord's Supper on which you feasted at that altar. You have the same Word of God, and the same Holy Spirit is present to work in your heart and renew your courage. You can turn to that Word daily. Even if the print becomes too small to read, you are not cut off from it. You can use a Bible with large print or listen to it recorded on cassettes or CDs.

Homesick for God's house? It is good that you feel this way. If this longing or hunger for the Lord and his Word would be absent, then an illness far worse than homesickness has set in, a sickness of the soul. But God has been faithful. He has kept you in his family. If for a time you must still be absent from God's house, he will come to you and keep your faith and your love for his house alive and strong until you move into that *most beautiful house of God*, never to be homesick again.

— *Prayer* —

Forgive us, Lord, for the times we have taken for granted the joy of entering your house to hear your comforting Word proclaimed. That joy is gone for now. Help us find the same joy in your Word as we read it or hear it, knowing that wherever that Word is, there the Holy Spirit is working his wonders in our hearts. Amen.

25

HE SPEAKS TO YOU WHEN YOU ARE BEING TEMPTED

Finally, be strong in the Lord and in his mighty power.
Put on the full armor of God so that you can take
your stand against the devil's schemes.

— *(Ephesians 6:10,11)* —

We might imagine that temptations should be less of a problem for us as we grow older. Sins that were so alluring to us as young people should no longer seem so attractive.

Let's not deceive ourselves. Satan becomes even more desperate to deceive us as our steps approach heaven. His temptations now are no less deadly than those of youth. No matter how old we become, we will still be engaged in a life and death struggle with the prince of darkness. It would be good to know what tactics Satan uses and what weapons we, in turn, need to overcome his temptations.

We dare not take Satan lightly. "Our struggle is not against flesh and blood, but against the rulers, against the authorities, against the powers of this dark world and against the spiritual forces of evil in the heavenly realms." (Ephesians 6:12). Every misery and evil in the world can be laid at the devil's feet, and he is not finished yet. He cannot overthrow God, but he does try to ruin God's garden, and he often does so with terrible success. He's won some of his greatest victories by convincing some people that he does not even exist and that they need not fear him. They fail to recognize that temptations come from him and that his intent is deadly.

His most effective tactic is still the one he used so successfully in the Garden of Eden: "Did God really say?" (Genesis 3:1). Even today he leads people to question God's Word. And those whom he has led into doubt include some leaders in the church. As a result, they proclaim from their pulpits messages that rarely speak of sin and grace. These doubters still refer to the Bible as God's Word but explain that the Bible is *about* God or it is a record of God's dealing with men or it *contains* God's Word. But then they also claim it includes *man's word* as well. They claim it is full of myths and legends and so it must be "demythologized." For them it is truth but often only poetic truth.

Satan attacks the individual tempting him with those sins that are most appealing to him just at the time when he is the weakest. Greek legend tells of a magical river whose water made people immune to injury. The mother of a boy named Achilles dipped her son into that magical river, as she held him by his heels, so no enemy would be able to wound her son. He never lost a battle until someone learned that his heels had not touched the water. Soon after, mighty Achilles perished, wounded by a poisoned arrow in his vulnerable heel. So Satan knows our Achilles' heel, our weak spot, and there he attacks us.

How can we hope to defeat such a mighty, cunning foe? Didn't Luther write, "With might of ours can naught be done; Soon were our loss effected"? Yes, but remember Luther immediately went on to say, "But for us fights the valiant one Whom God himself elected" (CW 200:2).

Winning the battle and achieving the victory do not depend on our strength. In fact, he who battled Satan for us at Calvary, and in that momentous battle crushed his head (Genesis 3:15), has already won the victory. "The reason the Son of God appeared was to destroy the devil's work" (1 John 3:8). As a result, we now know that we "have been set free from sin" (Romans 6:18).

Thus Paul writes, "Be strong in the Lord and in his mighty power." Use the weapons (described in Ephesians 6:11-17) that he has given us. Victory over temptation does not depend on our willpower or moral strength or determination. It is rather a matter of using the weapons God himself has provided for us.

Weapons, however, are useless to a soldier if he does not use them or if he leaves them in camp. We want to know the Scriptures well enough to call on a fitting word of God to use as a weapon when we are tempted, as Jesus did when he was tempted by Satan in the wilderness. Study the weapons God has provided, especially God's Word, and be alert to every temptation sent by Satan to destroy you. "Put on the full armor of God so that you can take your stand against the devil's schemes." Remember that God asks nothing of you without first giving you the strength to do it. And if you should fail, remember that Jesus didn't. By his overcoming all the devil's temptations, he is our perfect Savior. The victory remains ours in him.

— Prayer —

*Lord, give us strength to say no to every temptation.
We know that Satan is not a mythical figure but a
very real enemy bent on our destruction. He is alive
and well on the planet earth. May we face his fierce
temptations, armed with the strength of our Lord,
fitted with the weapons he has given us, and
comforted with the promise that he gives us the
victory he won for us once and for all times.
In Jesus' name we ask it. Amen.*

26

HE SPEAKS TO YOU AS YOU ARE TROUBLED ABOUT CHANGE

I am with you and will watch
over you wherever you go.

— *(Genesis 28:15)* —

Ours is a society on wheels. Nearly one of every four families moves each year—some just to the other side of town and others far across the country. This involves change, and change makes many people apprehensive. Perhaps we are experiencing the type of change where we must leave our home of many years and enter a rest home. The percentage of people who do that is surprisingly small, but we can't rule out the possibility that it lies in our future.

How might we react if this or other changes become necessary for us? Will they fill us with deep uncertainty and dread? In God's Word we find not only his promises always to go with us but also examples of people for whom changes brought great blessings—blessings they did not expect.

In our text we see Jacob setting out for the distant land of his uncle Laban. He had little peace of mind over this change.

He was leaving behind a father he had wronged and a brother who was furious enough to kill him. But God's promises went with him. He would go with Jacob every step of the way. In a vision of angels who were ascending and descending a ladder reaching to heaven, God gave Jacob peace for his conscience. In that vision he pictured the forgiveness promised in the Savior. At peace with God, Jacob could face any changes with confidence.

You know how Jacob's story turned out. God went with him and prospered him with dramatic miracles, so that Jacob returned to his homeland a very wealthy man, filled with reassurances of God's ability to protect and bless him.

Jacob's story is the rule, not the exception, in the way God works out changes for our good. Think of Abraham, called to leave behind his home and family for an unknown land. You are familiar with the blessings that this change brought to Abraham, as well as to us, since the Savior came from his descendants.

Ruth, the Moabite, lived through a drastic change when, in accordance with God's plans, she together with her mother-in-law, Naomi, traveled to what was for Ruth a strange land. When her future was bleak, another unexpected change took place. She was given a wealthy child of God for a husband, and as a result of that union, she became the ancestor of our Savior.

Or think again of Joseph and the drastic change that entered his life when his envious brothers sold him into slavery. Surely he would perish! But no! God went with him to Egypt and prospered him in a most wonderful and mysterious way.

The changes that happen in our lives may not be that dramatic. Maybe the blessings they bring will not be that obvious, but know this: the changes that lie ahead of us will be guided and controlled and blessed by our loving Father in heaven. If he sees fit to permit changes in our lives, he will use them for our benefit. His promise to Jacob is ours too: "I am with you and will watch over you wherever you go." He will bless us in whatever measure is right for us. He will keep his eye on us and see us through whatever changes may come into our lives.

The biggest and best change of all will come at the right time too, when he comes to welcome us into our everlasting home. Think of it! Forever with the Lord! What a happy and blessed change that will be! We will be freed of every misery, disappointment, and sorrow once and for all.

— Prayer —

Lord, I confess that I am uneasy about certain changes I face. I know that you are at the helm of my little boat of life. Lead me to be content to follow you on whatever paths you choose for me. Be ever with me. In Jesus' name. Amen.

27

HE SPEAKS TO YOU WHEN YOU NEED A MIRACLE

People brought to him all who were ill with various diseases, those suffering severe pain, the demon-possessed, those having seizures, and the paralyzed, and he healed them.

— (Matthew 4:24) —

Some situations seem utterly beyond hope. A doctor may have compassionately, yet bluntly, said as much. The X rays indicate that if there is going to be a recovery, it will take a miracle. Dare we actually hope for that? Aren't the days of miracles long past?

I'm certain that you are convinced that every miracle recorded in your Bible did take place in exactly the way it was written by those inspired writers of God. They recorded only what God told them to put down. Not once in the process did they err or lie or exaggerate.

So if Genesis tells us that in the beginning God needed only to say let there be and there was, we are content, knowing that this is exactly how the universe began. Or if God's Word tells us that the walls of Jericho simply fell to the ground without any human force being applied, we *know* this is how it was. The same is true of every miracle Jesus did while he walked among men.

But a miracle for us today? We don't question for a moment the Lord's ability to work one for us. We also understand that, in a sense, they are no longer needed. The miracles of Bible times, recorded by eyewitnesses guided by the Holy Spirit, have proved their point. They have served their purpose.

Take, for example, the miracles where Jesus healed the blind man and the ten lepers. Those miracles were not merely to give temporary relief from physical needs that could arise again. The lepers, delivered from their leprosy, probably faced other illnesses, as did the man born blind. The disciples, delivered from that storm on the Sea of Galilee, faced other storms. Lazarus, miraculously raised from the dead, died again. But the miracles did for them what Jesus intended. They were unmistakable signs that Jesus was their Savior.

Those miracles were recorded then, not only to show what Jesus can still do for our bodily needs, if necessary, but also "that you may believe that Jesus is the Christ, the Son of God, and that by believing you may have life in his name" (John 20:31). Miracles, in other words, were not just wonders to draw people's attention. They were signs, and we still have those signs before us in our Bibles.

In our dark hours, then, when only a miracle can help us, we need but revisit the scenes of those miracles—miracles that were performed also for us—to be convinced that Jesus *not only* has the ability to deal with whatever need faces us but also that he is our Savior, our Redeemer, our Lord, the same yesterday and today and forever. Can he help? Rather we should ask, "Is anything too hard for the Lord?"

Could our needs be too different from those of ancient times for us to dare hope for such help? Notice that God had dozens of miracles recorded. These he did not do just for the sake of emphasis or repetition. Each of the miracles dealt with a slightly different situation. All this is to assure us that whatever kind of miracle we need is within Jesus' power. If our welfare demands it, we will have it. And if no miracle seems to come, that too is just as much a wonder of God's love, as he continues to work out his purposes for us.

You feel you need a miracle to survive? Then pray boldly for it. But leave the issue in the Lord's hands. He knows better than you do what you really need. What assurance that gives you, to know that if you are asking something of God, you can expect him to do what is best for you, to do something even better and wiser for you than you may think to ask. Remember that his wisdom never fails. He never makes mistakes.

— *Prayer* —

Lord, sometimes we face situations for which only a miracle will do. Reassure our anxious hearts with the certainty that the age of miracles is still now, that you will never run out of wonders, that if our situation requires a miracle, it will come. Amen.

28

HE SPEAKS TO YOU
ABOUT HIS ANGELS

*He will command his angels concerning
you to guard you in all your ways.*

— *(Psalm 91:11)* —

Many people believe that the very idea of angels is preposterous. They consider the thought of relying on their protection as being hopelessly out of date. We pity those who feel that way. Even sadder, however, is the fact that there are Christians who as little children learned about and believed in angels, but who fail to realize the comfort they could have because of what God has revealed about them.

How about you? I am certain you believe what God has spoken about his angels. But do you ever actually think of them in times of danger? Do you feel more secure because you know that God has given them charge over you, to keep you in all your ways? When, in fact, did you last thank God for his angels and their ministry to you?

If only one Bible verse spoke about God's angels and their activities, that would be sufficient for our faith. But God speaks over and over about them and what they do in our behalf.

Just what do we know about them? They are spiritual beings. They are countless. They are wise and powerful. They are holy and cannot sin. They are God's agents to watch over us. They have served God as his messengers. We recall that God sent angels with messages to a wide variety of people—to Mary and Joseph, to Abraham, to Paul, to the shepherds, and to women at the tomb. In all these ways, angels have served God and man in the past and continue to do so in the present. As for the future, angels will gather the elect at the second coming of the Lord.

But what is it that they actually do in the present? First of all, angels surround us constantly to protect us. They stand between us and Satan, our fiercest enemy, to check his vicious fury. Our text reveals that God has given his angels charge over us to guard us in all our ways.

What comfort it is for us as parents and grandparents to know that angels care for our little ones. We could never watch our children closely enough, all the time, to keep them from harm. Luther once called angels "their angels" and added that were it not for the protection of angels, no children would grow to full age, even if their parents took all possible precautions for them.

Angels act in behalf of God for those who are older as well as for little ones. He sent an angel to warn Joseph of the vicious purposes of Herod against the Christ Child. Centuries before that, an angel held shut the mouths of vicious lions to protect Daniel. An angel also appeared in the fiery furnace and delivered the three young men from the flames. On another occasion, God sent just one angel into the camp of the Assyrians to destroy 185,000 men of war.

One favorite Bible story about the angels shows us that, although we do not see them around us, they and their protection are real. A Syrian king was seeking the life of the prophet Elisha, and early one morning Elisha's servant awoke to find himself and his master surrounded by the vast Syrian army with their glistening horses and chariots. His knees shook in terror, but Elisha calmly told him, "Those who are with us are more than those who are with them" (2 Kings 6:16). So that his servant might share his own peace of heart, Elisha prayed that the Lord would open his servant's eyes so that he could see the army of protecting angels that had been there to protect them all along. "He looked and saw the hills full of horses and chariots of fire" (2 Kings 6:17). God's mighty angels were on the job, and his children were safe.

For the same reason we can feel secure. We can pray with Luther, "Let your holy angel be with me, that the wicked foe may have no power over me." Trust God's promise about his angels, and laugh in the face of danger. For "the angel of the LORD encamps around those who fear him, and he delivers them," says the Lord (Psalm 34:7).

Thank God for his angels!

— *Prayer* —

How secure we can feel, dear God, knowing that if necessary, you could send legions of angels to our rescue! Though we cannot see them, remind us constantly that they are always around us to protect us. Amen.

29

HE SPEAKS TO YOU
ABOUT CONTENTMENT

*I have learned to be content
whatever the circumstances.*

— (Philippians 4:11) —

As you look around at the people you meet, you probably find some that always seem content and happy and others who just never seem satisfied. The strange thing is that some who seem to have every reason to be cheerful may be the very ones constantly complaining and grumbling. And those who possess the least reflect a kind of inner peace and contentment. Little annoyances just don't seem to bother them. They've learned the secret of true contentment. How they set an example for us!

Do you let little things spoil your contentment? When a meal is late, when a paperboy throws the paper into the bushes, when an appointment is forgotten, is that enough to ruin your day? Or on a more serious note, do you sometimes feel that even God is treating you badly—not giving you what you deserve or not seeming to care whether you are happy or not?

Paul reminds us that "godliness with contentment is great gain" (1 Timothy 6:6). He suggests that contentment goes along with godliness and trust. Let's look carefully at the text for this meditation. We hope that some of Paul's contentment may rub off on us as we come to understand why he feels as he does.

Note the words "I have *learned* to be content." Paul wasn't that way by nature. He had to learn this, and so can we. Let's let Paul be our teacher for a moment on the subject of contentment.

In previous verses, Paul had expressed his joy over a gift that his beloved Philippian Christians had sent him to meet his needs. It wasn't the gift itself that had made him so happy. He knew that God could and would take care of his needs. Rather, Paul rejoiced because this gift demonstrated that the faith of the Philippians was healthy and bearing fruit.

Then Paul says, "I am not saying this because I am in need" (Philippians 4:11). Rather, in Jesus, Paul already had everything that he could need. He was convinced that his Savior would not let him suffer for want. He would give Paul much or little, depending on what he knew was right for Paul. In Christ, Paul had everything to make him rich—rich even for eternity. In addition, prayer gave him the key to the storerooms of heaven.

Paul's contentment is no mystery to us, because it is how every Christian feels in some measure. His contentment demonstrates his faith and trust.

In my ministry, I came to know many a child of God who reflected that trust. One was a woman in her late eighties who was almost destitute. She kept her food cold by crawling down the steep steps with it each day to store it in the cool basement. She stayed fairly warm in winter by making that same exhausting trip down the stairs several times a day to get oil and then carry it upstairs for her space heater. One day when I called on her, she joyfully showed me a check sent to her by a distant relative for her birthday. With a happy smile, she insisted that I must take it for the Lord's work. "I don't need this money. I don't need anything. I have Jesus!" What an inspiration she was to everyone who knew her!

Have you learned her secret? You have if you remember that you too are God's beloved child whom he cherishes and protects and sustains. He gives you wisely and lovingly just what you really need. You don't have to worry what will happen to you. That's God's problem. You are his child. His love gives you total security, whether your bank account is healthy or sick. You don't depend on *things*; you depend on *God*.

When you are inclined to be dissatisfied, just look to Calvary and see how far God will go to give you what you need. What you possess is what he has chosen for you in perfect wisdom, just what is right for you. So you can be truly content. May Paul's attitude be yours in ever-greater measure, and may you, in turn, teach contentment to others by your example.

— *Prayer* —

Lord, help us find and reflect such a measure of contentment and peace that others will wonder at our attitude and be ready to listen as we explain the reason for the joy and contentment we have found in our Savior. Amen.

30

HE SPEAKS TO YOU ABOUT BUILDING ON HIS PROMISES

"God is not a man, that he should lie;
nor a son of man, that he should change
his mind. Does he speak and then not act?
Does he promise and not fulfill?"

— *(Numbers 23:19)* —

Broken promises are a dime a dozen, so to speak. We have all been deceived by the media, by politicians' promises, or by certain friends. At times we may even have been unintentionally deceived by our parents, who in all sincerity made promises to us, promises that they unfortunately discovered they could not keep.

Through experience we have learned not to put too much stock in the promises of people. Whom then can we trust? Whose promises are absolutely reliable? You know the answer, of course, from the Bible and from your own experience. It is written, "Not one word has failed of all the good promises he gave" (1 Kings 8:56). We are of course talking about the promises given to us by our God himself.

As our text puts it so simply and yet so eloquently: "Does he speak and then not act? Does he promise and not fulfill?" In other words, God is absolutely able to keep every promise and absolutely unable to break even one of them!

What a comforting reassurance that is for us who rely on those promises! The writer to the Hebrews also assures us that it is impossible for God to lie: "We who have fled to take hold of the hope offered to us may be greatly encouraged. We have this hope as an anchor for the soul, firm and secure" (6:18,19). The point is clear. If God makes us a promise, we can bank on it!

Another wonder of these promises of God is how they cover every area of our lives. We cannot hope, on one page or even many, to cover them all, but a partial list will convince you of the complete "coverage" they give you: He will never leave you nor forsake you. He will give you the peace of forgiveness in Christ. He will answer every prayer in perfect wisdom and love. He will guide, protect, and sustain you. He will make all things work for your good. He will give you strength to bear what needs to be borne, also in your years of aging. He will give you the precious gifts of the Holy Spirit through his "power tools," the means of grace. He who gave you faith will keep you in that faith and give you a believer's end. He will take you home to be with him eternally.

All these promises are nailed down by the fact that the one who simply cannot lie or err or exaggerate spoke them to us. So with Paul we can firmly say that we are "fully persuaded that God had power to do what he had promised" (Romans 4:21).

Do we doubt and make a liar of God? The problem with most of us is not that we doubt God's promises but that we at times forget them or fail to use them. Perhaps you have heard the tale about the flock of geese that would gather every Sunday morning to hear a sermon. They would marvel to hear how wondrously God had created geese. They could soar for miles above the earth, avoid all enemies, and see beautiful sights. Devoutly the geese would listen to this marvelous message, but then, after thanking God for his marvelous gifts to geese, they would waddle back to their mud holes for another week without giving a thought to flying. Life, you see, was much too comfortable for them as it was. There was no real danger at the moment, so why bother to fly?

Does this tale make us a bit uneasy? We gather on Sunday morning to hear God's wondrous promises and to hear about God's wondrous gifts. We believe and accept them. But then we return to our homes and little has changed. We forget the wonder of forgiveness, the power of prayer, the certainty of God's protection and care, the wisdom he's offered us in his Word. He has promised us the ability to soar in faith like eagles, but too often we flutter about as on broken wings.

Remember always the promises of God. They will never fail. Use them every day. Teach them to your children and grandchildren. You will soon learn the peace of building on God's gracious promises.

— *Prayer* —

No matter how unbelievable and awesome are the promises you have given us, Lord, may we ever trust them and wait for their fulfillment. Amen.

31

HE SPEAKS TO YOU ABOUT THE WORD OF THE KING

Since a king's word is supreme, who can say to him, "What are you doing?"

— *(Ecclesiastes 8:4)* —

Many times we Christians feel helpless to do the things we would like to do as God's children. We would so like an unwavering faith that never doubts. We'd like to get rid of our bad habits, to face life without whimpering and feeling sorry for ourselves, to depend always on God's promises, to forgive those who keep wronging us. Even the great apostle Paul knew that feeling: "For what I do is not the good I want to do; no, the evil I do not want to do—this I keep on doing" (Romans 7:19).

Where can we find the help to be what the Lord wants us to be? Consider now what Solomon says in our text. It would seem self-evident that when a king gives a command, his subjects jump to obey. They don't stand around and argue. They don't question his command. They don't hesitate. They *do* what their king commands. "A king's word is supreme."

94

But what is this saying to us? The writer is speaking not only of an ordinary king and his commands. He is talking about the King of kings. He is telling us that the Word of *this* King is packed with power to accomplish extraordinary things—the power, in fact, to do the impossible.

Consider a few examples of this power of the Lord's Word. We think immediately of creation, when God simply said, "'Let there be' . . . and there was" (Genesis 1:3)—mountains, oceans, stars, everything in the universe. Throughout the Old Testament, we witness the power of the Word of the King. He called forth out of dry rock water sufficient to satisfy the thirst of about two million people and their livestock. He spoke, and the waters of the Red Sea divided. He spoke again, and the sun stood still for Joshua and his army.

In the fullness of time, when the King walked among men for some 33 years, it was continually apparent that "a king's word is supreme." "Be opened," he said (Mark 7:34), and a deaf man could hear. "Lazarus, come out!" he commanded (John 11:43), and Lazarus came out of his tomb alive and well. To the paralyzed man, he said, "Get up, take your mat and go home" (Matthew 9:6), and the man did. He said to his enemies in Gethsemane, "Let these men go" (John 18:8), and the disciples were safe.

But it is in matters of the soul that we are most in awe of the power of the Word of our King. Paul called this Word a power of God, a dynamic force that works wonders in the hearts of sinners. It makes the spiritually blind to see, the deaf to hear, the dead to live. That Word turns sinners into saints and slaves of Satan into the children of God.

That amazing Word touched your life with its awesome power already at your baptism, when in a moment you became a new creature. All things became new. You were instantly a child of God. That Word, which created faith in you then, has sustained your faith since then. It has opened your eyes to see your Savior ever more clearly as the remedy for your sin. It has filled you with peace and comfort and joy and understanding. What a powerful word is the Word of the King!

You can depend on that Word in every spiritual need. When you need comfort, it actually works that comfort in your heart, as it also works love, peace, hope, joy, and the desire to follow and serve Jesus. Seek that word whenever you need these gifts. Let the Word of the King work in you what you would like to be and do. It will never fail you. Above all, it will keep your faith alive to the end.

— *Prayer* —

We know that you are almighty, Lord, but one thing you cannot do. You cannot lie or break your promises. May we ever trust your Word. Amen.

32

HE SPEAKS TO YOU WHEN YOUR GOD SEEMS TOO SMALL

"Is anything too hard for the LORD?"

— *(Genesis 18:14)* —

A famous Bible scholar made this shocking statement: "Your God is too small." How could he say something so ridiculous about God? How could God be too small for any task? Who created the universe with a simple command? Who divided the waters of the Red Sea to provide a dry path for his people? Who brought water out of a dry rock in mighty streams sufficient for several million people and all their cattle? Who made the sun stand still for Joshua? Who could rightly say to Sarah, when she laughed skeptically at the message that she and Abraham would have a child in their old age, "Is anything too hard for the Lord?"

How could that Bible scholar suggest that such a mighty, majestic God could ever be too small for even the least of our needs? Actually, he was saying something we all need to hear, that it is not God who is too small but *we* who are too small—too small in our conception of God.

The world has whittled God down to a man-sized deity whose word can be ignored and whose commandments can be trampled underfoot. And we too, in desperate times, forget how great he is. When our faith ought to be soaring like eagles, it flutters badly, and we become afraid.

Let's admit it. Our faith does not always soar in carefree flight. We forget what our protector is like. We tend to think of our Lord only in terms of the 23rd psalm, as a gentle shepherd who truly loves his sheep but is, perhaps, not quite up to the modern dangers and ailments of our day. Is God, we wonder, perhaps too small for our times with all their dangers, temptations, challenges, and changes?

In chapter 40 of Isaiah, the prophet paints quite another picture of the Good Shepherd in whom we trust. After describing him as a gentle shepherd who tenderly gathers lambs in his arms, the prophet shifts gears to show us the majesty and awesome might of that same shepherd, the Creator-God, "who has measured the waters in the hollow of his hand . . . [and] weighed the mountains on the scales and the hills in a balance" (verse 12). While "the nations are like a drop in a bucket . . . he weighs the islands as though they were fine dust" (verse 15). Then he pictures the Good Shepherd as a *mighty shepherd* of the heavens, who nightly leads the huge, countless stars out into the blue pastures of the skies. "He . . . calls them each by name. . . . Not one of them is missing" (verse 26).

That should give us food for thought about our conception of the God in whom we trust. Is he too small for our needs? How utterly senseless! We feel ashamed to have acted at times in our despair as though we cannot depend on his might.

How easily he can lead and protect and care for us as sheep of his flock. How fortunate we are to be the sheep of such a shepherd, the children of such a God, who is never, not ever, too small to meet our needs, whose love can never be indifferent to our problems.

No, the God we worship is never too small. Listen to the awe in Paul's voice as he cries out in wonder before the wisdom of God, "How unsearchable his judgments, and his paths beyond tracing out!" (Romans 11:33). Absolutely no problem is too complex for him, no crisis too difficult to solve. Protecting his own is child's play for him. We exult with David: "The LORD is my shepherd, I shall not be in want. . . . I will fear no evil, for you are with me" (Psalm 23:1,4).

When you are anxious and worried, remember this unassailable truth: The God we worship is *never* too small!

— *Prayer* —

How awesome you are, O God, in every aspect
of your being, your love, your might, your wisdom,
everything about you! Let us never foolishly act as
though you were too small for our needs. Amen.

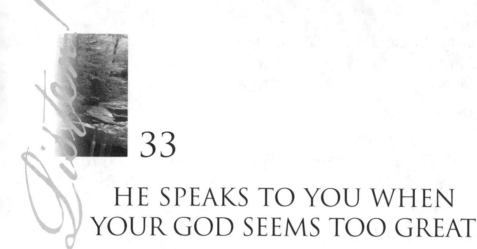

33

HE SPEAKS TO YOU WHEN YOUR GOD SEEMS TOO GREAT

I stand in awe of your deeds, O Lord.

— *(Habakkuk 3:2)* —

We can understand that some people could find themselves in such an impossible situation that they might imagine that their God is too small to help them. But to say that someone's God is *too great* really seems senseless and foolish. Don't we need a God whose wisdom and might are simply beyond our imagination? Isn't that the only kind of God who could possibly help us? How could one have a God who is too great?

Well, God's people, gathered at Mount Sinai to receive the law, were overwhelmed with such a feeling. They were overcome before this display of the majesty of God. They could not even bear to hear his voice.

Something like that happens to some people today when they read of the mighty deeds of God in the Bible. A hopeless feeling grips their hearts. They feel that God is just too great for them to dare to call upon him, too great to be expected to notice them, too holy to be able to understand their weakness and sin, too far above them to be bothered with their troubles. How could the Creator God, the Lord of the universe, be aware of their petty problems? How could he notice the sickbed on which they lie? They reason that he must be far too busy with the big things of the universe—the control of the billions of stars and the rise and fall of nations—to take time for little creatures like them. Too busy to be bothered with their aches and pains and to notice their whispered prayers amid the billions that rise daily to his throne.

The truth is that Jesus was never too busy to be concerned about even the lowliest of the people who came to him for help. He was not too busy to stop at Jacob's well to bring peace to a guilt-ridden Samaritan woman or too busy to turn that funeral procession of the widow's son at Nain into a joyous celebration of life. The almighty Son of God, by whom all things were made, took time to be born of a lowly virgin, to walk in poverty among men, to eat with publicans and sinners. Paul writes of him: "Being in very nature God, [he] did not consider equality with God something to be grasped, but made himself nothing, taking the very nature of a servant, being made in human likeness. And being found in appearance as a man, he humbled himself and became obedient to death—even death on a cross!" (Philippians 2:6-8).

Although he was mighty enough to break the chains of death, he was not too high and mighty to speak personally to Peter and to Mary. Nor is he too majestic to be concerned about you and me. The psalmist wrote, "I am poor and needy; may the Lord think *of me*" (Psalm 40:17).

Yes, God calls me friend. My name is written in the palm of his hand. The very hairs of my head are numbered by him.

I was in his heart already in eternity, in his thoughts and plans when he chose me to be his own. Small, unimportant, unworthy me, he loved enough to carry that cross. Mighty as he is, he is not too mighty—too far above me—to watch over my bed while I sleep, to have compassion on me and weep with me in my misery, or to be happy in making me joyful.

So the majesty of my God does not create *fear* in my heart but calm *peace* and happy *trust*. I do not run and hide from him as Adam and Eve did when they sinned. I run to him with joy, taking all my cares to him, as a child who has fallen might take his bruise to his mother to be kissed and tended. I don't have to shout for his attention. He hears my weakest prayer, even when it never gets spoken. I need never wonder if he is near, for I know that he is closer than any loved one could be.

Rather than worrying whether God is too great to forgive and protect you, rejoice in his greatness. It is your comfort and hope. Carry his invitation in your heart, "Come to me, all you who are weary and burdened, and I will give you rest" (Matthew 11:28). Remember that he calls you by name and says, "You are mine" (Isaiah 43:1). No, your God is not too great, but he is always great enough.

— Prayer —

Great and mighty God, we sometimes tremble before your majesty, as the Israelites did at Sinai. Help us remember that equally awesome are your mercy, your patience, and your love. Then your mighty power will not frighten us but will reassure us as we face the worst of enemies with the exultant cry of those slaves in Babylon: "The God we serve is able to save us" (Daniel 3:17). Amen.

34

HE SPEAKS TO YOU IN TIMES OF STORM AND STRESS

He replied, "You of little faith, why are you so afraid?" Then he got up and rebuked the winds and the waves, and it was completely calm.

— (Matthew 8:26) —

Listen to this sailor's prayer: "Lord, your sea is so vast and my boat so small; please watch over me and keep me safe." Isn't that the way we too sometimes feel—that the sea on which we are sailing is just too big for our little boat and that it is certain to be swamped? The disciples had that feeling, even though they were experienced sailors and knew from daily experience both the Lord's love for them and his ability to deal with any kind of storm. We hear them cry out in terror: "Lord, save us! We're going to drown!" (Matthew 8:25). Christians can have that feeling too, as they confront the storms and stresses of life.

While we all experience the violent storms in nature—when winds howl and lightnings flash and thunders crash—the storms that most threaten our little boat of life are of a different nature. They do not involve a raging sea but some stormy situations in life—illnesses that keep getting worse, bills that keep piling up, family problems that threaten our peace.

Forgetting who we are—God's own children—and who is protecting us—the Lord himself—we disregard all those past experiences when the Lord delivered us. And in the midst of our newest troubles, we are tempted to shout with the disciples: "Lord, save us! We're going to drown!" It is almost as if we were challenging God and saying: "Lord, don't you care about this terrible danger that threatens my life? What about all those promises you made to keep me safe? Where are all those promises now?"

Do you think we ever, ever, have the right to feel that way? Surely the disciples were not justified in their fear. It may well have been the worst storm they had ever experienced, but didn't they have one mightier than the fiercest winds and waves right with them in the boat—one in whose company they had always been secure? Little wonder that Jesus was disappointed in them. Just hours earlier, they had witnessed evidence of his almighty power in the feeding of more than five thousand people.

How often would he have to show his divinity before they would finally be ready to trust him? Even if he had permitted them to sink with their boat, he would not have been forsaking them. He would not let them perish. Surely they should have known that. Sadly he said, "You of little faith, why are you so afraid?" In his great patience, he did not turn away in disgust and anger, rather, "he got up and rebuked the winds and the waves, and it was completely calm."

Do you and I learn from this? When a fierce storm blows its way into our lives, however terrifying it might be, we want at once to remember who is with us in the boat of life. To help us cast aside all fear, we want to recall the many times he's helped us in the past. The storm was no problem for our Lord, was it? He needed only to speak a quiet command to those howling winds and instantly the sea became as smooth as glass. The waves had to lie quietly at the feet of their master.

That master is our Jesus, the same yesterday and today and forever. Those miracles related in the Bible are also there to quiet our anxiety, as should our own experiences with his help in the past. As someone has put it, "Our faith should always argue from the past to the present."

A hymn writer urges, "Let not faithless fears o'ertake us; Let not faith and hope forsake us" (CW 422:2). God's arm will never become too short to help nor his ear too deaf to hear our cries for help. Let us ever keep our eyes on him in the storm and wait for him to bring us quiet and peace. He will do that. Has he not told us so?

— *Prayer* —

As the winds of trouble howl around us, dear Lord, may we find peace of mind by turning to you with the prayer of the disciples. At the right time, speak to those disturbing winds, and they will lie helpless at your feet. Amen.

35

HE SPEAKS TO YOU WHEN YOU QUESTION GOD'S JUSTICE

[Our God] is the Rock. . . . All his ways are just.

— *(Deuteronomy 32:4)* —

Many centuries ago, King David wrestled with the same problem that bothers us at times. Why do the wicked so often seem to prosper and do well, while some of God's most faithful children seem always to be in difficulty? As David saw it, the ungodly prospered, but the health of the faithful children of God was poor and their crops were failing. Asaph wrote, "I envied the arrogant when I saw the prosperity of the wicked" (Psalm 73:3).

We've all witnessed situations that seem to involve injustice on God's part—when his ways did not seem just or fair to us. For example, I read about an incident that happened long ago to a Lutheran congregation in New York City. For their annual church picnic, the members chartered a large boat and set off for a day of special fellowship and praise. A sudden storm blew up, and the boat sank. In moments, an entire congregation of over a thousand members had lost their lives. One can well imagine how the godless of the city mocked the God who had permitted this tragedy. They questioned his love for his people, his ability to protect them, and, above all, his justice.

How might we have answered them? What do we say when tragedy, perhaps on a smaller scale but none the less tragedy, touches our lives? A fine young father dies and leaves a large family without a breadwinner. A young mother is taken, leaving her children motherless. A faithful church member retires and full of hope and joy moves into a new home, only to watch the house burn to the ground a week later. Dare we argue that God was just in such cases?

With what simple finality that question about God's justice is answered for us in our Bible. Moses needed only five words to do so, and we would all do well to ponder them and to keep them in our hearts: "All his ways are just." *All* his ways, not just *most* of the time, but *always.*

We don't expect to always recognize what God does as justice. His ways are so much higher than our ways and so far above our understanding. His purposes are often hidden from our eyes for the time being. So the purpose that lay behind the cross of Christ was for a time hidden from Peter. As a result, he tried to turn Jesus aside from any thoughts Jesus had about dying on the cross, as he had announced would happen. Peter did not yet understand that Christ's death on the cross would lead to his eternal life.

We don't need to understand God's purpose. We need to trust him. We can simply rely on this truth: God is just. He will not treat his children unfairly—not ever. He has a plan and purpose that he is working out for us. That is all we need to know. He has promised that one day we will look back, and then we will understand and praise him for what we at the time might have thought was not fair or just.

What a comfort this is for God's children! Remember Eli, who in his misery could still say, "He is the LORD; let him do what is good in his eyes" (1 Samuel 3:18). Recall Job's words: "Though he slay me, yet will I hope in him" (13:15). Job lost his children, his great herds, and his health. Yet he could say, "The LORD gave, and the LORD has taken away; may the name of the LORD be praised" (1:21).

Our hymnal includes many fine hymns written by people who had that same kind of trust in God's justice and love in their own lives and who captured it in their lyrics. The great hymnist Paul Gerhardt suffered endless sorrows. He lost his congregation. He followed the caskets of his family to their graves. Yet he wrote some of the most joyous hymns of trust in our hymnal. Not one word do we find in his hymns about any injustice on God's part. Only and always do we find words telling of God's faithfulness, mercy, and truth.

When it seems as though God is not treating you or some other faithful Christian fairly and justly, simply cling in faith to these three words: God is just!

— Prayer —

*When life seems unfair, help us understand,
dear Lord, that the problem is not with your justice
but with our faulty, limited vision. Because your ways
and thoughts are as high above ours as the heaven is
high above the earth, we cannot always understand
them. May we never accuse you of dealing unfairly
with us. When we cry "Why me, Lord?" may it not
be in foolish complaint but in awe and wonder
that we who deserve so little receive
so much from you. Amen.*

36

HE SPEAKS TO YOU IN THE DEPTHS OF YOUR LONELINESS

"Have not I commanded you? Be strong and courageous. Do not be terrified; do not be discouraged, for the LORD your God will be with you wherever you go."

— *(Joshua 1:9)* —

Nobody has a monopoly on loneliness. A little child may be terribly lonely, as may an unpopular teenager or a person who has lost his or her spouse. In fact, each stage of life has its own particular brand of loneliness.

Loneliness, however, may be an almost inevitable by-product of aging. Friends who once played a major role in the lives of older people have died or moved away or simply lost contact. The elderly may also be less and less involved in social joys, in the workplace, and in church activities. Their children gradually have moved out of the nest to make their own homes and lives. Often they live so far away or they are so busy that the elderly rarely get to see them or their grandchildren. The result is loneliness. No one stops by to see how they are doing. No one asks their opinions or advice or offers help with little tasks that seem to become bigger with each passing year.

God speaks to the elderly about this burden. He offers an escape from loneliness, an escape emphasized and repeated many times in Scripture. "Surely I am with you always" (Matthew 28:20). "Never will I leave you; never will I forsake you" (Hebrew 13:5). So also the promise of today's text: "The LORD your God will be with you wherever you go." The point is that no matter where you are—even if you were at the bottom of the ocean in a submarine or if you were miles above the earth in a space ship—the Lord would be there with you.

Yes, Jesus withdrew his visible presence from the disciples when he ascended into heaven, but he is just as surely beside us now as he was with them when he walked the dusty roads of Palestine. The disciples might have felt all alone and on their own after his ascension had he not promised, "Surely I am with you always."

We need not be lonely, even when we walk through the valley of the shadow of death. We can say with the psalmist, "I will fear no evil; for you are with me; your rod and your staff, they comfort me" (Psalm 23:4). We need never feel lonely, for our best friend is closer to us than any human being could be. His reassuring voice is as close as the Bible in our hands. His help is but a whisper away.

An ancient map of North America, dating back to 1523, hangs in the British Museum. Over certain areas, some unknown hand had written frightening comments, "Here there be fiery scorpions; here there be dangerous giants and dragons." Years later, a Christian scholar crossed out all these superstitions and wrote in bold letters across the entire map, "Here is God!"

Your future is like a map with many unknown paths. As you venture on any of these paths, you can put your finger on any date of the calendar of your future and write boldly: "Here is God! I shall not be alone!"

You may have heard of the poem by Mary Stevenson in which she tells of dreaming that she is walking along a beach with Jesus. The shore is marked by two sets of footprints in the sand. Glancing back, she is puzzled to notice that at times there is only one set of prints, and she asks the Lord, "Why, when I needed you most, have you not been there for me?" The Lord explains, "The years when you have seen only one set of footprints, my child, is when I carried you."

That inspiring poem did not quite express the whole truth. Along the entire path there would have been only one set of prints, the Lord's. At all times, easy and hard, he carries us. We are never on our own.

Alone? You are *never* alone. Put your hand in the Lord's. Listen for his voice and relax. Leave all things in his hands.

— *Prayer* —

Dear Lord, sometimes we feel alone in a world that seems too busy to notice us or care that we are troubled. May your Holy Spirit strengthen our conviction that we are never alone, that wherever we go, you are there to guide and uphold us. Amen.

37

HE SPEAKS TO YOU WHEN YOU FORGET YOUR THANK-YOUS

Jesus asked, "Were not all ten cleansed?
Where are the other nine?"

— (Luke 17:17) —

Most of us have been exposed to the bitter taste of ingratitude. Having gone all out to send someone a very special gift, we perhaps waited eagerly to hear that it had brought the delight we had intended and hoped for. But we received no word that it had even been received, let alone enjoyed and appreciated.

Thank-yous are important. Without them we remain uncertain whether our gift was a wise choice. Without them we lose the joy of being sure we have made someone we love happy. Without them we, unfortunately, have to assume that the gift meant little. As Shakespeare put it, "How sharper than a serpent's tooth it is to have an ungrateful child."

Far more serious is our frequent reaction of indifference and unthankfulness to God for all his gifts and daily kindnesses, as though such things mean little to us or as though God owes them to us. So much has God done for us that were we to spend the rest of our lives in constant hymns of thanksgiving, our debt of gratitude would barely be touched. How the Lord feels about this is clear from the many times he calls on his children to give thanks. He urges, "Give thanks in all circumstances" (1 Thessalonians 5:18), and he has given us a prayer many people use at mealtime: "Give thanks to the LORD, for he is good; his love endures forever" (Psalm 107:1).

Have you wondered why God is so concerned about thank-yous? Why should thankfulness be so important that he repeatedly has warned us about forgetting to give thanks? "Be careful that you do not forget the LORD," he says (Deuteronomy 6:12).

Why should God care? He whom angels in heaven praise for his gift of salvation to us hardly needs our weak, discordant hymns of thanks. They must sound like mere noise compared to the hallelujahs of the massed choir of angels. He will surely survive our ingratitude. He'll be none the poorer if we forget to say thank you.

The point is, God doesn't need our thank-yous, but we do. To be unthankful shows that we are not totally aware that all we have comes from him in grace, that we fail to realize our unworthiness for the least of his gifts, that we are blind to the wonders of his mercy and grace. Worse, it suggests that we have the attitude that he owes us what he gives. Possibly it even suggests the thought that we deserve even more than we already have.

This attitude not only dishonors God; it also harms us. Recall the sadness Jesus expressed when nine of the ten lepers who had been healed failed to return to thank him, even though his act of healing had given them a whole new life. "Were not all ten cleansed? Where are the other nine?" he asked.

He was not disappointed for himself but for them. They needed so much more from him than bodily healing, and he had so much more to give them. He wanted them to have healing for the wounds of their sin. He wanted to give them the very mansions of heaven, but they went their way, leaving these greater blessings untouched. By failing to return with a simple thank-you, they cut themselves off from the greatest of treasures he had for them. Having missed the opportunity, they would probably never get to know Jesus as their Redeemer, as their deliverer from sin and hell. In the long run, they would be little better off for his gift of healing.

So it is important for us not to forget our daily thank-yous. We owe them and we need them. Let's count our blessings every day and never give Jesus cause to say about us, "Where are the other nine?" Once we are truly aware of the lavish, extravagant kindness of God, especially his daily forgiveness, we will surely follow the sound advice of the apostle Paul: "Always [give] thanks to God the Father for everything, in the name of our Lord Jesus Christ" (Ephesians 5:20).

Thank you, Lord, for the reminder!

— *Prayer* —

We know, dear Father in heaven, that you can get along without our praise and thanks, but we also know that we can't. Help us recognize all your gifts and mercies and return to you with eager words of thanks and with hands open to receive all the other blessings with which you will enrich our lives. Amen.

38

HE SPEAKS TO YOU
WHEN HE SEEMS FAR OFF

You are near, O LORD.

— *(Psalm 119:151)* —

How small the world has become! News from even the most distant countries reaches us almost instantly. Planes take people across the ocean in hours. Even the moon is close enough today for people to visit.

On the other hand, science is discovering just how truly immense the universe actually is. It is so huge that distances between stars must be measured in light-years. The sun, an ordinary star in size, is yet so huge that if it were hollowed out, it would hold a million earths.

How small, indeed, we seem by comparison! And our God is over all those distant stars, controlling their paths and holding them in their places. We may wonder whether he might just be too distant to hear our weak, tiny cries for help. How far away he may seem at times when we need him.

We've told you about the Bible scholar who wrote a book called *The God You Worship Is Too Small.* In that book he was actually suggesting that our conception of God is far too limited, that we haven't even really begun to realize his greatness.

That same author could have written another volume with the title *Your God Is Too Far Off*—not for a moment implying that God is *actually* too distant to help us or even be aware of us and our troubles. But this time he could gently remind us that sometimes, when surrounded by difficulties, we are tempted to *think of* God as being far off, somewhere out in space, too distant to hear our cries, too far off to hear our pleas for help or our shouts of praise.

If that is our picture of God and his relationship to us, then once again we might begin to think or to act as if there were little or no use in depending on his concern or help.

Some people might find comfort in the thought that God is too far distant to notice the way they lead their lives. If that is the case, they reason that they can afford to be a bit careless.

For us Christians, though, the mistaken concern that God is far off might rob us of the precious assurance of knowing that the very God who is holding those stars in their precise courses is *never* distant from us, not even an inch away whenever we need him. David, for example, could go out fearlessly to do battle against Goliath only because he *knew* the Lord was not distant—that God, indeed, was fighting at his side. David could face his enemies knowing that "God is our refuge and strength, an ever-present help in trouble" (Psalm 46:1).

In their confirmation classes, our children learn that God is omnipresent, which means that he is everywhere, always present with us wherever we go, whether at home, on the highway, in the airways, in the shopping mall, in the workplace, or in the hospital—absolutely everywhere. The psalmist speaks of this in Psalm 139: "Where can I go from your Spirit? . . . If I go up to the heavens, you are there; if I make my bed in the depths, you are there. If I rise on the wings of the dawn, if I settle on the far side of the sea, even there your hand will guide me, your right hand will hold me fast" (verses 7-10).

This truth about God's omnipresence makes all the difference in the world for you, the difference between hope and despair, between terror and peace of mind. Let it never be a concern to you that perhaps your God is too far off, too far away to notice your burdens or to hear your cries for help. He is at your side, and you can face anything that life throws at you. A beautiful little prayer that you may have learned as a child summarizes this comforting truth: "Be near me, Lord Jesus; I ask you to stay Close by me forever and love me, I pray" (CW 68:3).

— *Prayer* —

Lord, help us realize that you are never too far off
to hear our whispered prayers, to see our needs,
to sympathize with our sorrows. We will fear
no foe with you at hand to bless. Amen.

Thirteen

39

HE SPEAKS TO YOU ABOUT COUNTING YOUR BLESSINGS

Praise the LORD, O my soul; all my inmost being,
praise his holy name. Praise the LORD, O my soul,
and forget not all his benefits—who forgives
all your sins and heals all your diseases,
who redeems your life from the pit and
crowns you with love and compassion,
who satisfies your desires with good things
so that your youth is renewed like the eagle's.

— *(Psalm 103:1-5)* —

With all its problems, the United States is still the envy of the world, a land of abundance, a land whose harvests are so bountiful that they sometimes pose a problem to farmers by depressing prices. One farmer put it this way: "Nature is killing us with kindness."

However, many of our readers, including farmers, are not living in abundance. Their incomes are low, perhaps even near the poverty level. They may need a new roof or furnace or barn and not have the money to afford it. Can we expect these people to join the psalmist in his hymn of praise as he counts up all his blessings?

What would our Lord say today to such struggling Christians? Perhaps he would use the words he spoke to Christians in ancient Smyrna: "I know your afflictions and your poverty—yet you are rich!" (Revelation 2:9). Or he might remind them of those treasures that make them eternally rich in that precious gift he sent from heaven wrapped in swaddling clothes, his Son, who "though he was rich, yet for your sakes he became poor, so that you through his poverty might become rich" (2 Corinthians 8:9).

The ancient prophet Habakkuk recognized the value of such a blessing. He wrote, "Though the fig tree does not bud and there are no grapes on the vines, though the olive crop fails and the fields produce no food, though there are no sheep in the pen and no cattle in the stalls, yet I will rejoice in the LORD, I will be joyful in God my Savior" (Habakkuk 3:17,18).

That prophet knew of a treasure that could not be measured in dollars. He had an understanding of values similar to that of the pearl buyer in Jesus' parable who came across the one perfect pearl and gladly sold all his lesser pearls to possess it.

That pearl—Christ—is why we can call Christians rich— rich way beyond the athletes and actors with their million dollar salaries. In the Savior we have total security, access to almighty help, peace with God, and the sure hope of spending eternity with him in heaven.

Paul so often reminds us that we are *in Christ*. To illustrate what this means, put Jesus in a big circle with everything he is and has and does. Then see yourself in that circle with

Jesus—see that he is yours, all he has is yours, all his truth and mercy and might are yours and have been ever since the Holy Spirit gave you faith and wrote your name in that circle with Christ. That is what it means to be in Christ.

How could anyone be better off than that? God calls you blessed, and that is what you are.

We have learned not to measure our wealth in terms of possessions. They may be nice, but they are terribly shaky and temporary. There is not one of them we could not lose in the next three minutes! When the chips are down, they mean nothing at all.

"A man's life does not consist in the abundance of his possessions," said Jesus (Luke 12:15). A Christian who holds fast to this truth remains a mystery to the world. He is happy not only over what God has given him but happy in spite of what God withholds, even happy because of it. Indeed, God gives and withholds in the same amazing mercy we learned about on Good Friday.

Picture our psalmist sitting quietly by himself and counting up his blessings. Suddenly he can't be quiet anymore. Words of praise and thanks break forth from his lips, "Praise the LORD, O my soul." Count your blessings and treasures in Christ, and the words of Psalm 103 will surely become yours also.

— *Prayer* —

Protect us from shameful unthankfulness, dear God. Move our hearts every day to count our blessings, especially those won for us at Calvary, and then move us to reflect this spirit of thanksgiving with daily thanks-living and praise. Amen.

40

HE SPEAKS TO YOU ABOUT LIFE'S MYSTERIOUS DETOURS

Oh, the depth of the riches of the wisdom and knowledge of God! How unsearchable his judgments, and his paths beyond tracing out!

— *(Romans 11:33)* —

Motorists are not happy to see a detour sign. It often means poor roads and lost time. Some detours, however, turn out to be pleasant surprises. They take us through unbelievably beautiful scenery that we would never have seen had we continued on the expressway. Sometimes we come across a quaint old village or a delightful restaurant, and we may decide that detours aren't so bad after all.

This is always the case with the spiritual detours you meet in your life, the changes in your course or plans that took you where you had not intended to go. Since it is your heavenly Father who charts your course, you really ought not to be surprised when these occasional detours turn out to bring pleasant surprises and amazing blessings. At the time, you rarely recognized this and you probably wondered where God was leading you. You were disappointed, and wondered why

God sent such a detour when things were going so smoothly and comfortably.

It is a good learning experience to look back at some of the detours on which God led his people in Bible times. We can discover how invariably they played into God's purposes and turned out for the best. For example, Joseph was sold into slavery, and a long detour took him to Egypt. At first that detour caused him concern and sadness, and it brought his father bitter tears. But as we look to the end of the detour, we see how it turned out to be just another of God's happy surprises. That detour resulted in the saving of God's chosen nation from drought and kept alive his plan of salvation.

That detour also protected God's people from the idolatry of their surroundings and prevented their extinction. In fact, this little family of about 70 people was so carefully protected and nourished in Egypt that a few hundred years later when they left for the Promised Land, they numbered in the millions. Their relationship with God was still intact in the promised Messiah. What a blessed detour that was—even for us.

An equally striking example of one of God's wise detours is seen when—after the plagues God sent to secure their release from Egypt's slavery—he led his people in the opposite direction of their goal. How they grumbled and complained, wishing they were back in Egypt! But that detour saved them from going through the land of enemies who were too powerful for them, and again, that detour kept the promise of the Savior alive.

God used detours, loving detours, also in the New Testament. The persecution that followed Stephen's murder caused the gospel to be carried to many lands.

Later, God led Paul on a detour to Macedonia. This turned out to be a mighty blessing for us. From Philippi—where he began his work in Macedonia—the gospel spread in every direction and eventually ended up right at our own doors and in our own hearts.

Perhaps at this very time you are being led on a detour away from the path you'd planned and anticipated. Perhaps your detour is a hospital bed or a nursing home. Trust God! These are detours he has carefully arranged. He knows where he wants to get you and how best to get you there. He will never choose purposeless detours or rough roads that are not necessary and serve you no good. He chooses the right road for you on your way to your heavenly home. Jesus has promised that one day we will look back over the road we have traveled, and we will recognize that every detour was the best thing that could have happened to us. Travel your detours cheerfully, trustingly. You will be delighted one day to see how they turn out.

— Prayer —

*May we remember always that the disturbing detours
of life are never by chance but are carefully charted
by you, our caring God. May we cheerfully follow
your leading. We have learned from your Word
that you have a plan for our lives. That is all
we really need to know. Thank you, Lord,
for the mysterious detours by which you
are leading us safely home. Amen.*

41

HE SPEAKS TO YOU WHEN YOU ARE ON YOUR KNEES

"Call upon me in the day of trouble;
I will deliver you, and you will honor me."

— *(Psalm 50:15)* —

Someone once said that the devil trembles when he sees a Christian on his knees. Something exciting happens when God's children call upon him in prayer. Maybe you are a veteran of years of prayer, having learned this art almost as soon as you could speak.

You understand already why you pray in Jesus' name. He made you and your prayers acceptable to God. You realize why you wisely add "if it be your will" when asking God regarding earthly needs, for what you ask may not really be a blessing.

You pray, convinced that no need is beyond his concern or ability to help, for he "is able to do immeasurably more than all that we ask or imagine" (Ephesians 3:20). You've learned that prayer is not a kind of last resort after all other help has failed, but, rather, it is the very first step you take.

You know that you don't need to reserve prayer for the big, dramatic needs in life, because no need is so trivial that your Lord is not concerned. Certainly the shortage of wine at Cana was not a life-or-death matter, yet he performed his first miracle there.

You are confident that you cannot come to God in prayer so frequently that you actually annoy and bother him, for he has told you, "Be alert and always keep on praying" (Ephesians 6:18).

You know that when an answer is not immediately visible, it is never because your prayer was not heard or that you asked the impossible of God. There is no *impossible* with him!

You are thankful that he will carefully evaluate your prayer and grant your request only if it is wise, so you need not worry about making foolish requests.

Some of the kindest things God does for us occur when he says no to some of our prayers. We would never really dare to pray if it were certain that God would grant everything we asked, because we do ask so foolishly at times.

Finally, you have learned to pray, "Lord, your will, not mine, be done; nothing more, nothing less, nothing else."

How tragic it would be if you were neglecting the awesome privilege of prayer and numbering yourself with those of whom James wrote, "You do not have, because you do not ask God" (4:2)!

For encouragement, search the Scriptures for examples of successful prayer. Elijah prayed that it might not rain, and "it did not rain on the land for three and a half years. Again he prayed, and the heavens gave rain" (James 5:17,18). Consider how astonishingly and lavishly Solomon's prayer for wisdom was granted. Read Jonah's prayer from the belly of the great fish, and see his faith in adding a song of praise to his prayer, even before an answer was apparent and help was on its way.

The Lord has not become too deaf to hear. Not even once has he broken his promise to answer prayer. No request you bring to him is beyond him. He could painlessly make all of us billionaires if that were right for us, and he would not be the poorer for it. He could give us all perfect health every day of our lives and yet not tax his strength. What he cannot do is fail to grant what we really need or fail to grant it when we need it. Nor can he grant what is unwise and harmful to us. And so we pray boldly, regularly, confidently, and gratefully.

If for a time you are too weak to put words together to form your own prayer, you will almost always remember and can always use the prayer Jesus himself gave us, knowing that what you need is covered in that prayer. The Lord's Prayer is like a big basket that contains all your needs.

Begin this very day, this hour, to make use of the awesome privilege of prayer that is yours as God's child. Take your problem to him and leave it there. He will know how to deal with it.

— *Prayer* —

Dear heavenly Father, once again we bring our burdens and aches to you in prayer. Knowing that you are greater than any need we have, we leave them all in your hands, trusting that you will know best how to deal with them and that you will surely do so. Amen.

42

HE SPEAKS TO YOU
WHEN LIFE SEEMS JOYLESS

Rejoice in the Lord always.
I will say it again: Rejoice!

— (Philippians 4:4) —

We've all known individuals who go through life with constant frowns on their faces, never smiling, looking as though they hadn't a thing in the world to be happy about. Other people seem to radiate a spirit of gladness, even though their homes are humble, their cars are old, and their health is a constant problem. Clearly such people know of a joy that lifts them above all these annoyances and problems, a joy nothing can touch. What a pleasure it is to be with such people!

A man like that, a man of positive joy, is speaking to us in the text for this meditation. Not only was his a joy no one could take from him, but he clearly expects you and me to share with him that *always* kind of rejoicing, that *always* happiness. That man, the apostle Paul, urges, "Rejoice in the Lord always." And to make sure we get the message, he repeats it, "I will say it again: Rejoice!" Paul is convinced that, as Christians, we have reasons to be joyful, whatever our circumstances.

How can Paul expect us to rejoice *always?* Doesn't he know about the sadness and disappointments that overwhelm our hearts at times? Was he perhaps writing from some "ivory tower" where all was pleasant? Not Paul! He'd been in prison for four years. He'd known enough suffering to fill a book. You can read of his experiences in 2 Corinthians 11:23-27, and see him beaten, stoned, shipwrecked, imprisoned, slated for a martyr's death. Yet after some 15 years of what most people would certainly consider misery—and this is what his faithful service to Christ brought him—his heart was so full of joy that in this very short letter he speaks of rejoicing no less than 17 times.

Paul could not expect an *always* kind of rejoicing in us if we were to look for it in things, in success, or in power. That would not be possible. It is an entirely different story, however, when Paul urges us to rejoice "in the Lord," for in him is a joy that can never be taken from us. We have the assurance that everything we really need in this life we shall have. We hold in our hands all we need for eternity, the key to heaven's glory and eternal joy.

Long before Jesus' birth, Sarah, the wife of Abraham, learned to laugh for joy over his coming. She foretold that in him all the world would one day laugh with her (Genesis 21:6). That prophecy comes true in the joy we find in Christ today, even when we are suffering. The apostle Peter writes, "Even though you do not see him now, you believe in him and are filled with an inexpressible and glorious joy" (1 Peter 1:8).

Some Christians imagine that life should be a "bowl of cherries" because they are God's children. No! Rather, the apostle Paul reveals God's will for us when he writes, "We must go through many hardships to enter the kingdom of God" (Acts 14:22). Even as the cross of Jesus was an absolute necessity for our salvation, so every cross and burden that touches our lives must be necessary, or God would not permit such things. He permits no unnecessary pain to touch our lives, and whatever sorrows we feel are in his control and must serve our good.

What happens to us in the end is what always counts with him, and that is what he has in mind as he charts the course of our lives. As we but catch a glimpse of the peace and joy that awaits us in the presence of Jesus, we agree that we have reason for an *always* kind of rejoicing. Rejoice in the Lord always, then, for yours is the joy that lasts.

— *Prayer* —

Dear Savior, may we never give anyone the impression that our lives are empty and joyless. May our faces reflect the peace and hope we have found in your salvation, and may our lives be a constant hallelujah of praise. Grant us the faith to rejoice in the Lord always. Amen.

43

HE SPEAKS TO YOU WHEN YOU NEED GUIDANCE

*Guide me in your truth and teach me, for you are
God my Savior, and my hope is in you all day long.*

— *(Psalm 25:5)* —

Already in youth life is filled with many difficult choices. In fact, we have to make many of the most vital decisions of life even before we are truly mature. We have to decide what school to attend, what courses to take, what profession to follow, whom to marry, where to live and work—all weighty choices indeed.

Difficult decisions, however, also pile up and confront us as we grow older. We need to make choices about when to retire, where to live, how to meet expenses, how to invest any savings we might have, and so forth. There is no end to the books and articles we could read on any of these subjects. Some are helpful and can be safely followed. Others, however, are dangerous and foolish to consider further, for the advice they give often directly contradicts God's Word.

Wouldn't it be great to have a friend of superior wisdom, a guide, a counselor, to whom we could go for good, solid advice for any problem that might arise? God speaks through the psalmist, who names the Lord as just such a guide: "You guide me with your counsel, and afterward you will take me into glory" (Psalm 73:24).

Here is the one guide for whom the future is an open book and who can tell us which way to choose, which paths to follow. For this guide there is "no dark place" (Job 34:22). Everything for him is as clear as day. No mysteries perplex him; no problems are too much for him. He always knows the wisest choices for us.

Looking to the Lord for such guidance, the psalmist wisely prays, "Guide me in your truth and teach me."

If the God of all wisdom has promised to guide us, then we need not stumble fearfully and desperately through life as though we were walking through a minefield. Our heavenly Father has charted our paths for us.

How does God guide us? In earlier times he spoke to men in visions. He guided the apostle Paul, for example, in just such a way. Through a vision he led Paul to put aside his intended mission plan and to journey instead with the Word to Philippi.

Today it is his Word that guides us. We can turn there at any time to find guidance that we need. With the psalmist we confess, "Your word is a lamp to my feet and a light for my path" (Psalm 119:105). That Word leads us to our Savior lying in a manger, and it takes us to the scenes of his miracles, his suffering and death, his resurrection, and his ascension. It is a totally reliable guide, because it is God's own Word, God's own revelation.

While a road map can only show us the right road, this Word of God goes a step further and moves our hearts to follow its light along the road of life and salvation.

The psalmist prayed, "Guide me in your truth and teach me." How desperately we need such guidance to God's truth today, when error occupies so many pulpits and runs rampant in so many religious books and articles! No doctrine seems safe from errorists today: not creation, not the prophecies, not the virgin birth or incarnation of Jesus, not his miracles, not his substitutionary death, not his divinity, not even his resurrection. Little is left of the Bible after it has filtered through their hands, except a human book about God, filled with human myths and legends and mistakes. Increasingly rare is the pastor who still bases his sermon on a clear "It is written" or "This what the Lord says."

The inerrancy of the Bible and its verbal inspiration are almost teachings of the past on the religious scene of our day. So the one dependable guide to truth has all but vanished and no longer directs people's thinking on matters such as evolution, fellowship, divorce, abortion, or homosexuality.

When people forsake the Word, what else can we expect? Then there are no more absolutes of truth—of law and gospel. Those who turn out the light that God himself provided are bound to walk in darkness.

We need not grope through life, however, as if in darkness. We have a bright light that guides us as unerringly as that special star guided those wise men to their Savior and ours. With David we say, "Guide me in your truth and teach me."

— Prayer —

We ask you, dear Lord, to lead us to choices that you would want us to make. Left to our own wisdom, we could only choose wrong paths. So we look to you, only to you, for guidance. Amen.

44

HE SPEAKS TO YOU ABOUT YOUR STRAYING CHILD

Train a child in the way he should go, and
when he is old, he will not turn from it.

— *(Proverbs 22:6)* —

Most mothers in the animal world are extremely protective of their young. They stand up ferociously against anything that threatens them. But sometimes they do become careless. Last week, for example, a mallard duck foolishly led her seven tiny ducklings not only down a high curb and up again in front of our home but even out into a busy street. She then wandered off with six of her seven "children," failing to notice that one very tiny baby duck was unable to negotiate the curb and had been left behind to fend for itself.

That incident, however, reminded me of how most mothers watch over their little ones. They barely let them out of their sight and would risk their lives, if necessary, for them.

All parents are given the grave responsibility of leading their children on the right path to Jesus. Most Christian parents, thank God, take that responsibility seriously. They don't stop being concerned, even after their young have left the nest and gone out on their own. Daily they wonder: "What company are they keeping? What place do they give God in their busy lives? Are they safe, really safe?" When they hear that one of their children is drifting from the Lord, they are heartbroken. How can they call such a child back to the Lord and his ways? How can they shake the bold confidence of such a youth if he or she refuses to listen?

It helps to remember that while God uses parents in the training of their children, saving souls is his business. Only he can work that wonder. The Lord, not we, kindled the precious spark of faith in the hearts of our little ones through his Holy Spirit. He who chose them for his own already in eternity sought them in Baptism and gathered them into his fold as his lambs. And he alone can keep them safely in his fold.

At the same time, God expects us to use our Christian influence on our children whenever we can—teaching them the right way by word and example. If they begin to stray in spite of us, we need not to give up on them but, rather, to turn to the Lord for help. Think of what he managed to do with the life of the persecutor named Paul or the dying thief or the Roman centurion at the foot of the cross. Each was brought to a bold confession of the Christ he had just met.

If our children should stray in later years, we can quiet our aching concern by remembering that the living seed of the Word was planted in their hearts at their baptisms. And although that seed may seem to be dormant for years, the same Holy Spirit who made it sprout in the beginning can make it grow and flourish again. The words we taught them are very likely still in their hearts and memories and may take hold again.

With joy we have witnessed many wayward youths brought to their senses and brought back to their Savior in some mysterious way. Perhaps it happened through an illness or accident or through a sermon heard at the funeral of a friend. We should never cease praying for those who have strayed.

As an encouragement, we can think of that dying thief whose situation seemed absolutely hopeless. Very likely he had been brought up in a good Jewish home where he had once memorized the promises of the Savior to come, but he had slipped into a life of crime. Yet, in his midnight hour, he was patiently sought and found by the dying Savior, from whose lips he heard that incredible promise: "Today you will be with me in paradise" (Luke 23:43).

That is why it is so important to "train a child in the way he should go," clinging to the promise, "when he is old, he will not turn from it." In your concern for a straying member of the family, take that person to the Holy Spirit in prayer, and leave the rest to God.

— Prayer —

*Gracious Father, how our hearts ache when we see
one of our loved ones forsake you and your ways.
Comfort us in the knowledge that though they
forsake you for a time, you will never forsake them.
Cause the seed once planted in their hearts, now
seemingly dormant, if not dead, to sprout again
and grow, so that they turn again to you
as their Savior and Lord. Amen.*

45

HE SPEAKS TO YOU WHEN YOU STRUGGLE WITH DOUBTS

"The Scripture cannot be broken."

— *(John 10:35)* —

It is Satan's greatest ambition to rob us of our faith. He wants to get us to doubt God's words and thus to drag us down to where he is forever. It is not surprising then that we meet with so many fierce attacks on our faith.

Satan's tactics have not changed much since the very beginning. He still loves to whisper in our ears the beguiling doubt he planted so successfully in the Garden of Eden, "Did God really say?" (Genesis 3:1). Does God really love you when he permits you to suffer such trials? Is his wisdom truly equal to any problem? Can he keep such incredible promises? Is God's Word really all truth, without any error whatsoever?

In confronting Satan's temptations on the words and wisdom and justice of God, remember first of all that the truths of God are so far above our human thoughts that we, on our own, cannot expect to understand them or even to believe them. It took a miracle of the Holy Spirit to give us faith that believes and trusts even what it can't understand.

That is not disturbing at all but, rather, comforting. If God and his ways were no different than ours—no better than ours—he would be or could be of little help to us.

Paul calls God's ways unsearchable, his judgments past finding out. He tells us that no man can plumb the depths of God's wisdom. So the creation story is incredible. That is great; it tells us how unbelievably mighty our God is. Likewise, the accounts of the wonders we meet throughout the Old Testament: the dividing of the Red Sea, the fall of Jericho, the standing still of the sun—these wonders do not disturb our faith; they strengthen it. They show us how great our God is.

So it is with the miracles of Jesus—turning water into wine, healing all the sick brought to him, walking on the water, calling Lazarus alive out of the tomb. Could Jesus actually have done these things? How can we be sure? Because God says so and God cannot lie. As Moses recorded, "God is not a man, that he should lie. . . . Does he speak and then not act? Does he promise and not fulfill?" (Numbers 23:19).

Attacking the truth of God's Word is obviously the key to Satan's attempt to rob us of our faith. He wants us to doubt the virgin birth, the miracle accounts, the reports of Good Friday and Easter. For if he can convince us that the miracles were nothing but myths and fables, or that just one word of the Lord is in error, then the Bible contains falsehoods and is no longer God's inerrant Word. Then we can never be certain again even about our forgiveness. Gone would be our conviction that the Bible is the verbally inspired Word of God, totally and absolutely true. No longer would our faith be unshakable and solid.

Today, "pious doubts" are the messages from all too many pulpits. Doubt is actually called the essence of faith by some. Then there are those preachers who still use the language of the Bible but empty it of all meaning. They agree with the expression that the Bible is God's Word, but they interpret it to mean only that it *contains* God's Word or tells about God. Jesus arose, they say, but not physically. He lives, but only in the lives and memories of his followers. Both Paul and Jesus were attacked by the thinking of their day. The Lord's Supper becomes only a memorial feast; Baptism does nothing but picture the washing away of sin. They speak piously and eloquently, and many are deceived.

Luther once remarked that you can't keep sparrows from flying over your head, but you can keep them from making a nest in your hair. So with doubts; we do have a way of driving them out of our hearts. We do so by staying close to God's Word. "If you hold to my teaching, . . . you will know the truth" (John 8:31,32). Some eight hundred times in the Old Testament, we are told, "says the Lord," and that makes every word absolute truth.

So let us never speak the language of doubters who say, "I think; I am fairly certain." Rather, with every prophet and apostle, let us always plainly say, "I know; I am convinced; I am persuaded." Face all doubts with the Word and a bold "Amen, so shall it be."

— *Prayer* —

O Holy Spirit, drive out all the doubts that Satan seeks to plant in our hearts about you and your truth, and give us a joyous trust in your Word. Lord, we believe; help our unbelief. Amen.

46

HE SPEAKS TO YOU WHO NEED ASSURANCE OF SALVATION

[The disciples] were greatly astonished
and asked, "Who then can be saved?"
Jesus looked at them and said, "With man this is
impossible, but with God all things are possible."

— (Matthew 19:25,26) —

In this age of anxiety, people are concerned with almost everything except sin and hell and their eternal future. Very few wet their pillows at night, as David did, with tears of remorse over their sins. In fact, one survey indicated that over 90 percent of all Americans feel that they are just about everything that God can expect them to be.

We might expect Christians, especially elderly Christians, to know better and to see the truth about themselves more clearly than most—to see themselves as God sees them, born in sin, daily sinning much, and indeed deserving nothing but punishment. But it is just at this critical time that Satan manages to confuse many. He tempts elderly Christians to look back at the fairly respectable lives they have lived, at the many dollars they have contributed to the church, and at their faithful attendance at worship in the past.

How often, for example, a pastor is saddened and shocked to hear a rather active member say on his deathbed: "Pastor, I'm not afraid to die. I've always tried to live by the golden rule and to do what was right. I'm confident that God will take me to heaven when I die."

Thank God that we have the Holy Spirit, who keeps us from such false security—keeps us from building our hopes for eternal life in any way, shape, or form on the "good lives" we have lived. With the Holy Spirit's help, we will continue to realize that, of ourselves, we are totally unworthy of heaven. We have not, of course, erased even the slightest sin by all our efforts.

When we hear the troubled words of the disciples in our text, "Who then can be saved?" we could easily share their despair had not Jesus continued to speak these assuring words to them and to us, "With man this is impossible, but with God all things are possible."

So salvation *is* possible, even for us, just as it was an assured reality to that dying thief to whom Jesus promised, "Today you will be with me in paradise" (Luke 23:43). The point is not that since God accepted such a wicked man into heaven, he will have to accept us too. Rather, it's that we have that same merciful Savior, who in pure grace has given us that same hope and promise.

"With God all things are possible," Jesus said, and we know what incredible miracles of grace it took to make our salvation possible. Our salvation is all God's doing. So the saints before God's throne remind us as they sing, "From the LORD comes deliverance" (Psalm 3:8). Salvation is his to give.

Nothing in regard to our salvation depends on us—not even the faith that has accepted God's free forgiveness. That was God's gift too, the result of his working in our hearts. He chose us in eternity, entirely by grace. He sent his beloved Son to pay the cost of our salvation, entirely by grace. He sent his Holy Spirit to work the wonder of faith in our hearts, entirely by grace. In that grace he has kept our faith alive to this very hour.

Now, not even Satan can condemn us for the sins we have committed, for "There is now no condemnation for those who are in Christ Jesus" (Romans 8:1). "Though your sins are like scarlet, they shall be as white as snow; though they are red as crimson, they shall be like wool" (Isaiah 1:18).

We won't always feel forgiven, but God's words are clear. When we are distressed by some sin in which we have been enslaved, Paul reminds us, "Whenever our hearts condemn us . . . God is greater than our hearts" (1 John 3:20). And our Lord himself tells us, "Take heart, . . . your sins are forgiven" (Matthew 9:2). So then it is not false confidence or pride when you exult, "I know I am going to heaven," for this is the assurance you have from God himself.

— *Prayer* —

Gracious Father, you have assured us that we are your redeemed children by faith in Jesus. May that confidence be ours all through life, to the very moment we close our eyes in peace. To that end, bless our hearing and reading of your Word. Amen.

47

HE SPEAKS TO YOU ABOUT HIS "LITTLE THEOLOGIANS"

Even the sparrow has found a home, and
the swallow a nest for herself, where she
may have her young—a place near your altar,
O LORD Almighty, my King and my God.

— *(Psalm 84:3)* —

We are not all bird lovers, but few of us fail to appreciate the flashing beauty of a cardinal, the song of a wren, or the soaring flight of an eagle. As the heavens declare the glory of God and all nature shows the beauty of his handiwork, so our feathered friends proclaim the wonders of God's creation and teach us many lessons. Luther once called them "God's little theologians," suggesting that we should listen to the lessons they teach us about our God.

For our first lesson, we look to the mighty eagle. Moses writes, "Like an eagle that stirs up its nest and hovers over its young, that spreads its wings to catch them and carries them on its pinions. The LORD alone led him" (Deuteronomy 32:11,12). An eagle stirs up her nest—makes it uncomfortable—in order to force her young to get out and learn to fly. But she hovers over them every moment, and the moment they are in trouble, she rushes to hold them up and protect them. So the Lord "stirs up our nest," permitting afflictions to come and make it uncomfortable for us. But at the same time, he continues to hover over us, always ready to come to our rescue and save us.

While an eagle could teach us still other lessons, let's turn to the worthless sparrow to learn an even greater truth. The sparrow mentioned in our text had learned a vital lesson. If it built its nest at the side of the altar in the temple, it was safe. There it could confidently hatch its young. Even though that sparrow was surrounded by the violence of the sacrifices and the death of animals, with blood flowing down the sides of the altar, it was safe there—no one would touch it.

Here we learn a most comforting truth. As long as we build our lives at the altar of the cross of Christ—though it too was the scene of violence, with blood flowing freely—we are absolutely safe there from the accusations of Satan and our consciences. Even the consequences of our sin cannot touch us there, for "the blood of Jesus, his Son, purifies us from all sin" (1 John 1:7). What a lesson we learn from the lowly sparrow! We are to build our lives and hopes at the cross.

This little theologian, the sparrow, has other lessons to teach. In the Sermon on the Mount, we hear it sing its happy, untroubled song without a trace of worry, as if it knows it has a heavenly Father watching over it. In applying this lesson to us, Jesus said, "You are worth more than many sparrows" (Matthew 10:31).

God's little theologian teaches us to forget our cares and worries about food and earthly needs, even our sin and guilt, for we have a secure nest at the cross of Jesus. Paul writes,

"Therefore, there is now no condemnation for those who are in Christ Jesus" (Romans 8:1). By the same act in which he restored peace with God for us and made us members of God's family, he removed our anxiety about earthly needs. "He who did not spare his own Son, but gave him up for us all—how will he not also, along with him, graciously give us all things?" (Romans 8:32).

See God's loving care for a lowly swallow, guiding it thousands of miles each spring to its nest. Surely then we can trust his loving concern and care for us whom he bought at such an awesome price at Calvary to be his very own.

As we watch God's little theologians every day and hear them sing for sheer, carefree joy, in simple trust, let's take to heart the lesson they teach us for our own lives: leave all things in God's hands.

— Prayer —

Thank you, heavenly Father, for the birds
of the air, which teach us the lesson of cheerful
trust in you. Help us remember that we are of more
value than all the sparrows in the world, for it was
for us that Jesus died and rose again. Amen.

48

HE SPEAKS TO YOU ABOUT
YOUR GOOD SHEPHERD

The LORD is my shepherd, I shall not be in want.

— *(Psalm 23:1)* —

When the best-selling novel *The Man Nobody Knows* was first published, many wondered who was the main character referred to in the title. Was he a famous scientist or musician so wrapped up in his work that he chose to cut himself off from the world? Or was he, perhaps, some recluse? Just who *was* "the man nobody knows"? You've probably already guessed that the author was writing about a man everyone *seems* to know, the most famous man who ever lived: Jesus Christ.

But why would the author speak of Jesus that way, as the man nobody knows? As you read the book, you come to the conclusion that the author wanted to make clear that some of today's theologians (though they've written learned books about Christ in which they deny his divinity, his virgin birth, his miracles, and his resurrection) *do not really know* the Christ of the Scriptures. Even those who call Jesus Lord and Savior, but do not trust him or his Word, obviously do not know him as well as they should, for to *know him* is to love him, to trust him, and to follow him wherever he leads.

Let's take a closer look at Jesus the Good Shepherd, so eloquently described in the 23rd psalm. He is that same gentle shepherd whom the prophet Isaiah introduces with the words "He tends his flock like a shepherd: He gathers the lambs in his arms and carries them close to his heart; he gently leads those that have young" (40:11). You can't read these words and not see the loving concern this Shepherd has for us, his sheep.

But some may wonder whether such a mild, gentle shepherd is actually powerful enough to protect his flock and to feed and care for them. Isaiah shatters such concerns by vividly portraying another side of this Good Shepherd. "Who has measured the waters in the hollow of his hand, or with the breadth of his hand marked off the heavens? Who has held the dust of the earth in a basket, or weighed the mountains on the scales and the hills in a balance?" (40:12). See then what an awesomely mighty shepherd our gentle shepherd actually is!

Listen as Isaiah enlarges on this thought, "Lift your eyes and look to the heavens: Who created all these? He who brings out the starry host one by one, and calls them each by name. Because of his great power and mighty strength, not one of them is missing" (40:26). So the gentle shepherd of Psalm 23 is also the Creator of all things. He is the *mighty shepherd of the skies,* who nightly leads the huge stars out into the blue pastures of the heavens, as a shepherd might lead his sheep. He calls each of the billions of stars by its name. Not one is ever missing or lost.

Knowing this about him, we begin to get a more complete picture of the Good Shepherd and truly get to know him in whom we put our trust. We who have seen the beauty of his love see also the glory of that power by which he broke the chains of death for us at Easter. We see him 40 days later as the King of kings, ruling all things with our welfare in mind.

Yes, God's children find much comfort in the 23rd psalm. We know why we can confess with David, "I shall not be in want." We walk through the valley of the shadow of death without trembling, because the presence of our shepherd comforts us. That such a majestic shepherd can love us unlovable sinners is in some ways his greatest glory.

Early Christians would picture Jesus on the walls of caves, not holding a lamb that anyone can love but a goat, the symbol of a most unloved, unwanted creature. The point they wanted to make is that Jesus loves *all* the sheep of his flock, also us, *even* us. Rest assured, then, that he loves you as though you were the only one to love. *All* his love is yours.

Praise the Holy Spirit that he has brought you to know and trust "the man nobody knows," both as the gentle shepherd of our daily lives and the mighty shepherd of the stars. Such a shepherd is surely to be trusted. Always. Completely.

— Prayer —

Holy Spirit, help us know more fully that love in which the Good Shepherd laid down his life for us, the power in which he protects his flock, the wisdom in which he guides us. May we remain his sheep until he brings us safely to our eternal home in heaven. Amen.

49

HE SPEAKS TO YOU
ABOUT HIS PROVIDENCE

"You intended to harm me,
but God intended it for good."

— *(Genesis 50:20)* —

An unbeliever fails to recognize God's hand behind any event. For him everything happens by chance. It's all a matter of good luck or bad. By contrast, God's children see his loving hand behind everything that touches their lives. They know that nothing just happens—nothing is just accidental with the Lord. Not even a sparrow falls from the sky without his knowledge.

Happy events for Christians become even happier. They know that these blessed times come from a loving heavenly Father, who delights to see them filled with joy. Disappointments are not only more tolerable, but they become reasons to give thanks to God. He permitted these disappointments to happen in the same wisdom he demonstrated in creation and in the same perfect love he planned Calvary.

Some Christians accept sorrow in what they *choose to think of* as Christian resignation. Their attitude, however, reflects more of a hopeless stoicism in which they accept misfortune because there is nothing they can do about it anyway. In the meantime, they really feel that they could have planned things much better themselves.

True Christian resignation means leaving things in God's hands. It means being thankful that he has made wise and loving choices for us—sometimes momentarily painful but, nevertheless, what we need. Maybe it is something that we would never have had the wisdom or courage to choose for ourselves. Christian resignation is simply trust in God's ways and accepting his ways as infinitely better than ours.

The life of Joseph is a beautiful demonstration of God's providence at work. Sadness certainly filled his heart when his envious brothers sold him into slavery, but he did not despair. Even though at the time he could not see what God had in mind for him, he trusted God's plan for his life. We, who know Joseph's complete story, can readily recognize God's purpose as it unfolded. God turned Joseph's seeming tragedy into a mighty blessing for him, for his whole family, and for the whole world, even for us.

Because Joseph came to see God's controlling hand, he could easily forgive the evil act of his brothers, saying, "You intended to harm me, but God intended it for good to accomplish what is now being done, the saving of many lives" (Genesis 50:20).

The Bible is filled with inspiring examples of God's providence at work in the lives of his children. Recall how he chose a Jewish girl named Esther to become queen of a heathen kingdom in order to deliver his people. Remember how he led Caesar Augustus to set his whole empire in motion so that God's promise of a Savior might be fulfilled exactly where and when God said it would happen.

Recall how bloody persecutions scattered the early Christians and so caused the spread of the good news of Jesus. The blood of the martyrs became the seed of the church. Wherever the Christians fled, they took the gospel with them. As always, God brought good out of that evil. From the mission work carried out by those persecuted Christians, the gospel eventually came all the way to our country, our towns, our homes, and our hearts.

That amazing providence of God is as active in your life today as in the time of Joseph. He has an exciting plan for your future and is working out that plan to perfection! When sadness touches your life, don't lose faith or become bitter. Thank God for the good he will bring out of evil for you. His plan will have the happiest of endings, the brightest of futures. Wait patiently and trustingly. Remember that God works in a mysterious way his wonders to perform, and one day you will look back and say, "He has done all things well."

— *Prayer* —

O Lord, give us quiet confidence in the wondrous providence in which you plan and control every event in our lives. Help us always to know and believe that because of your guidance, all things must work together for our good. Amen.

50

HE SPEAKS TO YOU AS YOU STRUGGLE TO FORGIVE

Then Peter came to Jesus and asked, "Lord,
how many times shall I forgive my brother
when he sins against me? Up to seven times?"
Jesus answered, "I tell you, not seven
times, but seventy-seven times."

— (Matthew 18:21,22) —

It is not easy to forgive, especially when you have been wronged over and over again. Can God really expect you to do so? Is it actually that important that you forgive others?

Turn the question around. How important to you is God's forgiveness of your sins? Would it matter that much if you had no forgiveness? It surely would! Without the forgiveness of your sins, you would not be God's child. You would have no peace with God, no right to pray, no hope that God is for you and with you. Without forgiveness you would have no help to fight sin, no hope of escaping hell or experiencing the joys of heaven.

Obviously, God's forgiveness does matter in your life as, in fact, nothing else does. How vital God considered it! Think of how much he paid to make forgiveness possible. In view of all this then, consider the words of Jesus: "But if you do not forgive men their sins, your Father will not forgive your sins" (Matthew 6:15). What a terrible thing to do to ourselves—to refuse to forgive!

Yes, it is difficult. What can help us forgive those who have sinned against us? To begin with, understand that God expects it of us, his children. He repeatedly tells us to forgive. And in thankfulness for his forgiveness and all his other mercies, we will want to do just that in order to please him.

Peter understood this in part, but he wondered how often it was necessary for him to forgive. In his day, many thought that to forgive a person three times was quite enough. So to be on the safe side, Peter spoke of being willing to forgive seven times. Jesus answered, "I tell you, not seven times, but seventy-seven times." He was not saying that 77 times would be often enough. Jesus meant we are *always* to forgive! Peter was to remember the mountain of his sins against God, all freely forgiven, and to contrast that mountain with that tiny little pile of offenses someone may have done to him.

As Luther put it, "He *daily and richly* forgives all sins to me and all believers." That is why I want to be ready to forgive, because I have been forgiven so much, so many times by God.

Jesus brought this home to Peter by telling him the parable of a great ruler who graciously canceled the huge, insurmountable debt of one of his chief servants instead of selling him and his family into slavery as was his right. How angry this ruler became, however, when that same servant turned around and did just the opposite because of a pittance owed to him by a lower servant. That forgiven servant cast his

155

fellow servant into prison until he would pay his debt, a feat that he, of course, would never be able to manage while he remained in prison.

The ruler said: "You wicked servant, . . . I canceled all that debt of yours because you begged me to. Shouldn't you have had mercy on your fellow servant just as I had on you?" (Matthew 18:32,33). Then Jesus applied this to all Christians, "This is how my heavenly Father will treat each of you unless you forgive your brother from your heart" (verse 35).

So we are ready to forgive, not simply because it is demanded of us but because God has so graciously forgiven us. We know that he will take care of the offense done us; that is not our business. In fact, he can turn the harm that has been done unto us into a blessing. If God turns the evil into good, should it then be so difficult for us to forgive?

Why forgive? We do so "just as in Christ God forgave [us]" (Ephesians 4:32). Our thankful hearts will not permit us to do otherwise. Not only *must* we forgive, as Christians, but we *want* to do so. Forgiveness of others is our thank-you to God.

True, others may still not forgive you. It makes no difference. You are not an ordinary person. You, God's own forgiven child, are a forgiving child!

— *Prayer* —

**Dear Lord, help us forgive others
as you have so often forgiven us.
In Jesus' name we ask this. Amen.**

51

HE SPEAKS TO YOU
ABOUT HIS ATTRIBUTES

*Oh, the depth of the riches of the wisdom
and knowledge of God! How unsearchable his
judgments, and his paths beyond tracing out!*

— (Romans 11:33) —

A seminar of the world's greatest minds, meeting together for years, would not even come close to answering questions like these: Who is God? Where is God to be found? What is he like? The most powerful computer ever built would come no closer to supplying the answers. To the mind of man or any computer that man might invent, God is unknowable. As Paul put it, "Who has known the mind of the Lord?" (Romans 11:34). God is simply too far above us, both in his very being and in all his ways. And yet how desperately we need to know him!

How can we hope to do so? Graciously and patiently God has *revealed* himself to us, telling us all that we need to know about him in his Holy Word. He reveals himself to us as the triune God, and we know with certainty that while there is but one God, there are three persons: Father, Son, and Holy

Spirit. And while his ways too are beyond us, he has revealed what he is like in ways that we can understand.

Let's look at just a partial list of his attributes, as he has revealed them to us, trying in the process to see the meaning each one has for us. He is almighty. In other words, there is absolutely nothing too difficult for him to do. He is eternal, that is, without beginning or end. He is unchanging and will not suddenly change his mind about our salvation. He is omniscient—there is absolutely nothing that he does not know. Even our thoughts are like an open book to him. He is omnipresent—he is everywhere at the same time and so always beside us. He is holy, totally without sin. He is just, fair in everything he does. He is faithful, always keeping his promises, always able to keep his word and unable only to fail to do so. He is merciful, having compassion on us in our weakness. He is gracious, ever showing us love that we do not deserve. He is patient, bearing with us when we fall again and again. He is tender, dealing with us, in spite of his majesty and might, as a mother who cares for her child.

Paul in our text says that God's judgments and ways are unsearchable. And his love? We have found remarkable ways to plumb the depths of the ocean, but we never will find a way to plumb the depths of God's love for us. He loves every one of us as though there were but one of us to love.

Equally unsearchable and mind-boggling are each and every one of his attributes, and our listing is surely far from complete. A child can memorize a list of God's attributes in ten minutes, but to learn to use and apply them takes a lifetime. The more we think about them, the more they will help us get through the rough spots of life.

It is so easy to say that God is love but so hard to remember it when life is rough—to be convinced that he loves *you,* and that *everything* he does with your life reflects that love. We can talk ever so eloquently about his wisdom, but how quickly we sometimes wonder about that wisdom when he leads us on paths we don't enjoy. We call God just, but how unfair he seems to us when the wicked prosper all around us and the faithful suffer.

So we sometimes have to struggle to apply the attributes of God, which we ought to see as absolute facts, to our lives. God *is* love; he *is* just; he *is* almighty, and so on. Each one is a kind of building block in making our faith secure and solid.

Wouldn't it be a wise use of time for us to memorize that list of God's qualities and carry it with us, ready to apply it to any new situation that troubles us? What a help that would be! God's attributes are a powerful shield against all doubt and fear and anxiety, as an answer to any question that troubles us. They will not fail us, even as God himself can never fail us.

— *Prayer* —

***Lord, help us rely on all of your wondrous
attributes as building blocks in that foundation
on which our faith can rest securely
in every crisis. Amen.***

52

HE SPEAKS TO YOU WHO GRUMBLE ABOUT THE WEATHER

Sing to the LORD with thanksgiving; make music to our God on the harp. He covers the sky with clouds; he supplies the earth with rain and makes grass grow on the hills. He spreads the snow like wool and scatters the frost like ashes. He hurls down his hail like pebbles. Who can withstand his icy blast? He sends his word and melts them; he stirs up his breezes, and the waters flow.

— *(Psalm 147:7,8,16-18)* —

In this meditation we are not just talking about the weather; we are also talking about God's providence, which lies behind it. It is said that God's ancient people saw his hand in every event, while most of today's people see his hand in practically nothing.

For example, an ancient Persian king had a bridge of ships built to enable him to invade Greece. When a violent storm broke up his bridge of ships, furious with rage, he ordered his soldiers to give the sea three hundred lashes with chains. He blamed the sea for the weather.

When enemies of the Reformation came through the German countryside hunting for the followers of Luther whom they intended to imprison, they failed to see a little cottage occupied by Lutherans by the roadside. A heavy blanket of newly fallen snow was hiding it from their view. Saved from capture, the Lutherans thanked God for the heavy snowfall, because they saw it as part of God's providence to protect their lives.

Have you ever connected God with the weather? Do you see his hand in rain or snow? We hope so. We continually hear people complaining about the weather, and perhaps we do it too without thinking. Nothing with God is accidental, not even weather. When we complain about snow or rain, are we unconsciously and unintentionally criticizing the very works of God—questioning his love and wisdom? It is God who is behind the rain and the sunshine, always with a purpose. When we recognize this, we catch sight of the completeness of God's providential care of us, his people.

Where does weather come from? A forecaster may end his broadcast with the words "This weather comes to you courtesy of your local food stores," but he does not actually mean that. He is actually more scientific and attributes the weather to prevailing winds, barometric pressures, and so forth.

Could that mean that even we, God's children, are the helpless victims of impersonal storms and accidental tornadoes and that this is one area of life of which God is not in control?

God's purposes in the weather he sends us are usually hidden from our sight. It makes no sense to us when a tornado flattens a village, a hailstorm destroys the corn crop, or a storm at sea causes a ship to capsize. For example, it certainly had to look like the most awful tragedy when, in the early 20th century, a sudden storm off Manhattan Island sank a cruise ship loaded with almost 1,100 members of one Lutheran congregation. Instead of enjoying their annual church picnic on that chartered boat, they all perished in the storm. "If the Lord is behind the winds that blow, as the Bible says, where was he that day?" people asked.

What comfort to know from Scripture that it is our loving Lord who "supplies the earth with rain and makes grass grow on the hills. He spreads the snow like wool." This means that there was indeed a divine purpose in that tragedy.

What about us? Do we complain because the day is too cold or too hot, instead of leaving the weather in God's hands? Perhaps with a storm that frightens us, he is reminding us how small and helpless we are and how much we need him. During a soaking rain, he reminds us of the truth of his promise that he will continue to water the earth.

We need not always understand. It is enough to know that he is always in control, even of the elements, and that we can face bad weather or good weather with Eli's trust, "He is the LORD; let him do what is good in his eyes" (1 Samuel 3:18).

So we have yet another reason to praise God. We have seen even more evidence of the completeness of his providence.

— Prayer —

Help us, Lord, to recognize your hand in every kind of weather and to trust you to know when we need sunshine or rain. When storms disrupt our plans, may we remember that they too are part of your perfect plan for our lives and that they also serve your purpose of love. Amen.

53

HE SPEAKS TO YOU AS YOU ARE FOLLOWING A STAR

Magi from the east came to Jerusalem and asked, "Where is the one who has been born king of the Jews? We saw his star in the east and have come to worship him."

— *(Matthew 2:1,2)* —

How we all love the biblical account of that special star God placed in the sky to guide those wise men to the Christ Child. What a king this had to be, to have his own special star in the sky. What a child this had to be, to hold in his tiny hands the only hope for a sinful world. How fitting that the wise men brought gifts fit for a king, for a king he is, the King of kings and Lord of lords!

How richly blessed those wise men were to be given such a star to follow! How could they ever have hoped to find such a lowly child, born in poverty in tiny Bethlehem, without it? You and I are no less blessed. We have an even more amazing star of God to guide us to Jesus. It is the very "star" to which that star in the sky guided the wise men in their search for the birthplace of the king—the star quoted by the scribes in

Jerusalem, directing them to Bethlehem, the star of God's Word.

That Word still lights up our paths to Jesus and is "a lamp to [our] feet, and a light for [our] path" (Psalm 119:105). We have lived our lives guided by that star, and it has always given us safe and certain guidance. Because of that star of God's Word, we are his children and heirs of heaven.

When we were little, God provided lesser stars that he placed in our homes, our pulpits, and our classrooms to lead us to Jesus. Never in a million years could we have found that Savior by ourselves. Without that star of the Word, to which our parents, pastors, and teachers guided us, we would have been no different from those millions groping through life without Christ, without God, and without hope in the world. We would still be strangers and foreigners to God's kingdom, still on the way to an eternity of agony in hell.

Do we recognize the responsibility this places upon us? The shepherds returned home glorifying God for all that they had seen and heard. They simply *had* to share their thrilling experience of finding the Savior. So these wise men hardly could have gone home and forgotten all about their astonishing discovery in Bethlehem. They must have told and retold their story to anyone who would listen. Who knows how many heathen came to know the Savior through them and found peace with God in him?

Now, two thousand years later, the apostle Paul calls *us* stars whose privilege it is to guide people to the manger and God's Christmas gift. We want to "shine like stars in the universe as [we] hold out the word of life" (Philippians 2:15,16). We have the same incentive as the wise men had to do so, for like them, we are Gentiles, unexpectedly led to Jesus by God's grace. The story of those Gentiles is recorded for us that we might know that Mary's child was born for us too.

How can we shine as stars today? In *A Tale of Two Cities,* a man named Carton visited a friend who was in prison about to be executed. He managed to exchange places with that friend, so he was led out to be executed while his guilty friend escaped. He died that his friend might live. So much he loved him. His sacrifice rang a bell with another prisoner, causing her to remember someone she had known years ago—one who took the place of us guilty ones and died that we might go free. That man named Carton served as one of God's little stars to lead someone to Christ.

In less dramatic ways, we are stars for others today—by the words and acts that reflect our Savior and his love, thus bringing others the peace we have found in Christ. We do this out of love for them, but there is a special promise for us too as God's little stars: "Those who lead many to righteousness [will shine] like the stars for ever and ever" (Daniel 12:3).

— *Prayer* —

As that special star guided the wise men to you, dear Savior, may the bright star of your Word ever lead to you as our Redeemer and King. Amen.

54

HE SPEAKS TO YOU LIVING
IN THE SHADOW OF DEATH

*Precious in the sight of the LORD
is the death of his saints.*

— *(Psalm 116:15)* —

Nothing so terrifies most people as does the thought of dying. Ordinarily, they may be fearless and powerful people, but death is one enemy that is too much for them. Some of them will not even permit the word *death* to be spoken in their presence. For example, one of the wealthiest men in the world would not even attend the funeral of his own son, because he was so terrified at this reminder of his own mortality.

What a striking contrast to the attitude of God's children! Listen to the apostle Paul, who not only spoke serenely and calmly about dying, but even awaited it eagerly. It is a victory to be celebrated and a gain to be anxiously anticipated. "For to me, to live is Christ and to die is gain" (Philippians 1:21). Calmly Paul looked forward to death, as he says: "I am already being poured out like a drink offering, and the time has come for my departure" (2 Timothy 4:6). "But thanks be to God! He gives us the victory through our Lord Jesus Christ" (1 Corinthians 15:57). "I desire to depart and be with Christ, which is better by far" (Philippians 1:23).

Simeon is another beautiful example of how every Christian can feel about death: "Sovereign Lord, as you have promised, you now dismiss your servant in peace. For my eyes have seen your salvation" (Luke 2:29,30). Not a hint of fear or anxiety taints his words. Rather, there is an eagerness to die *now*. The exciting experience of being welcomed home by his Lord can't come too soon for him. We hear him praying for that moment.

I can hear you saying: "But these men, Paul and Simeon, are heroes of faith. What about common, everyday Christians like you and me?"

In my ministry I have stood at the bedsides of hundreds of people who were confronting their last hour. There I witnessed that same serene peace in the face of death so often that it no longer surprises me. It was the rule, not the exception! Will we, like Paul and Simeon and those countless others, face death with that bold attitude, or will we tremble?

Well, let's look into the heart of our loving heavenly Father for a moment and see how he feels about our dying. Will our deaths make him sad? Is it a defeat or failure of his plans for us? Or will he rejoice with his angels over a great victory?

In Psalm 116 God calls the death of his saints precious. Dare we, who sin so much, consider ourselves saints? If so, why should our death be precious to him who loves us? Obviously our lives are precious to him. We know that. But our deaths? Let's consider these two questions for a moment.

Remembering our sins and weaknesses, we may hesitate to think of ourselves as God's saints, for the word means holy ones. But we realize that God uses the word in a different way. To him, the word *saints* is not one that is applied just to the great heroes of faith in the Bible or just to the people who have lived particularly pious lives. Nor does he regard as saints only those Christians already with him in heaven.

Notice that the Bible makes it clear that a saint is one who has been sanctified, that is, made holy by the Holy Spirit, cleansed of sin by faith in Christ Jesus. A saint then is simply any believer in Christ, whether that individual is a pious old grandmother, a child just baptized, a leader of the church, or a dying thief. You, dear friend, are one of God's saints, and so your death is precious to him. Your death is not a tragedy. It is the moment of fulfillment for all of God's exciting plans for you in eternity.

Your death is your joyous homecoming hour. There and then you will be out of reach of all temptations, of all misery, and of all disappointments. You will move into your real home where there is never any more pain or sorrow. Of course that moment is precious to God. Think what it cost him! And because it is precious, it won't happen at just any time but at the time and in the manner he carefully chooses. Nothing with him is accidental, certainly not our joyous homecoming hour.

Do not let your heart be troubled at the thought of your homecoming, but be filled with eager anticipation and longing for what Simeon calls a quiet departing in peace, to be forever with the Lord.

— Prayer —

Sovereign Lord, may the thought of death hold no terror for us, but rather stir up our hearts' keen anticipation for the moment when you welcome us home to be with you forever. Amen.

55

HE SPEAKS TO YOU
AT THE LORD'S TABLE

Come to me, all you who are weary and
burdened, and I will give you rest.

— (Matthew 11:28) —

In whatever need we find ourselves, in any kind of problem or difficulty or trouble that confronts us, no question is as basic as this: "If God is for us, who can be against us?" (Romans 8:31). If he is against me, nothing can help, but if he is for me, nothing can harm me.

The fact that we are God's redeemed children ought to make our lives ever so secure and serene. The problem comes in, however, when our troubles start to pile up. Then we begin to wonder if God is really for us. We think of our many sins and wonder how our holy and just God could possibly be for us.

Even a beautiful sermon about God's grace and forgiveness sometimes doesn't quiet such misgivings. We sit surrounded by many people in the church service and wonder whether that message of forgiveness can possibly be meant *for us*. We simply feel too unworthy for such mercy. Just when we need assurance the most, because some critical illness or profound trouble has wedged its way into our lives, our uncertainty is the greatest. We are haunted by our sins.

Graciously and patiently God has provided a way to chase away such doubts and uncertainties. He has given us the Lord's Supper to fill our hearts with a wonderful peace.

Human eyes see nothing remarkable on the altar, just ordinary bread and wine. But the Lord has assured us that at his Table, we are partaking of a mighty miracle of grace. With that ordinary bread and wine, in a mystery far above our understanding, Jesus is giving us—in, with, and under the bread and wine—that very body and blood given into death for our forgiveness. He offers each one of us, his guests, the very price he paid to redeem us, his true body and blood given and shed for us for the forgiveness of sins. We know it is meant for us, for he says so. He deals with each one of us individually, one by one—given *for you,* poured out *for you.* We leave the altar with a clean slate and a conscience that is at peace. We leave, but the Lord goes with us.

If at times we do not feel forgiven as we leave the altar, we should remember that forgiveness is not a matter of emotions or feelings, but the certainty of the clear Word of God and the evidence he has just given us.

So we know that God is for us—that whatever may happen in our lives, we can make a fresh start, armed with the strength of our forgiving Lord. Those sins that caused us such uneasiness and guilt and feelings of unworthiness have been removed as far as the east is from the west.

Naturally we will want to receive the Lord's Supper often, both in bad times and good. But we need it especially in times of trouble.

What if you cannot commune in church because of a disabling illness that prevents you from attending? That need not and must not keep you from the joy and peace of the Lord's Supper. The sacrament is as close to you as the pastor is to his phone, and he will gladly commune you in your home. I know what that will mean for you. Countless members have told me after communing, "Now I feel so good. Now I feel forgiven. Now I feel at peace with God." What a tragedy it is when a Christian neglects a treasure like this!

Be the Lord's frequent guest, and you will know that same peace. Let me illustrate from my personal experience. I can recall communing one of my members who was dying. After he received the sacrament, he first expressed the peace he knew in Christ. Then he rose up on his deathbed and spoke the benediction over me, his pastor. He fell back and died. I had shared Christ's peace with him. He used his final breath to share Christ's peace with me. What a thrill that was!

— *Prayer* —

Dear Savior, we thank you for the peace that floods our hearts at your Holy Supper, as we receive the very price you paid to redeem us—your body and blood. May the Holy Spirit move us to come often and leave your table each time with a new comfort and with the deep certainty that all our sins have been forgiven. Amen.

56

HE SPEAKS TO YOU AS YOU KNEEL AT THE MANGER

Mary treasured up all these things
and pondered them in her heart.

— *(Luke 2:19)* —

There never was a gift like God's precious Christmas present, a child wrapped in swaddling clothes and lying in a manger. But why think of that today when Christmas might be many months away? What does that gift mean to us in July or October?

That gift touches every date on the calendar with comfort and peace in the knowledge that "God so loved the world, that he gave his one and only Son" (John 3:16). Gave him? For what reason? For what purpose? To be the centerpiece and theme of Christmas cards and carols and one-day celebrations? NO! The miracle of the manger is immeasurably greater and more important than that.

It was the beginning of the culmination of God's incredible plan to save mankind from sin and hell. His Son would turn God's anger away from all of us by taking it upon himself. He would endure our suffering and die our death. All the unspeakable anguish of hell earned by all people would be heaped upon him, that one sinless man, on Good Friday.

That much God loved the world—that was the price he was willing to pay for our redemption.

Little wonder the angels sang hallelujahs, even though their joy was for us and not themselves. Little wonder the shepherds returned home, glorifying God for all that they had heard and seen. Little wonder that God's children laugh in joy as they celebrate the Savior's birth. That is the laughter of God's children at Christmas, the laughter of sheer relief and contagious joy and hope and gladness.

Sad to say, that is not the usual laughter of today's lavish Christmas celebrations. The "birthday child" is often missing from them. Sometimes even we Christians seem little wiser. Do we forget the wonder of Christmas even before the trees and lights have been put away for another year?

A famous skeptic was expressing the doubts of many people when he said of Bethlehem, "Nothing really happened there." Nothing? Nonsense! *Everything* happened there. God's own Son became the child of a lowly virgin so that you and I might become the children of God. He left heaven's glory for a time so that its doors might be opened wide for us as our eternal home. He came to be forsaken by his Father so that we in our need might never fear that God has forsaken us. He came to endure God's anger, which was ours by right, so that we need never suffer without the assurance that God is not angry with us. He came to die so that we might live eternally. He became what we were so that we might become what he is.

One other gift God included for us—Christmas faith. Without that gift, the birth and death of the Savior would not help us. That gift too is a miracle of God, and we want to cherish it.

Luther once said that the virgin's faith was as awesome as the virgin birth. What a wonder that this poor teenager could believe that God had chosen her to be the mother of the Savior, that her helpless baby (who needed to be fed, washed, and changed) was not only her Creator but her Redeemer, and that his tiny hands held the only hope for the salvation of the world!

God gave her wisdom too. She did not leave the manger behind. She "treasured up all these things and pondered them in her heart." How often she would need to remember the glories surrounding his birth that identified him as the Son of God, especially on Good Friday! Her Christmas memories helped her to know that Jesus was not a helpless victim of his vicious enemies but that he was the mighty victor, who accomplished exactly what he had come to do. His cry, "It is finished" (John 19:30), was like a battle cry of completed redemption. He had redeemed her. She was at peace with God.

Throughout the year there will be times when you also will need the memory of the glories surrounding that manger, identifying Jesus as your Savior. Store them up in your heart for such times as Mary did. Then the peace and hope of Christmas will always be yours.

— *Prayer* —

Oh, rejoice, all Christians, loudly, For our joys have now begun; Wondrous things our God has done. Amen. (CW 45:1)

57

HE SPEAKS TO YOU AS YOU LIVE IN THE EPIPHANY LIGHT

"I am the light of the world. Whoever follows me will never walk in darkness, but will have the light of life."

— *(John 8:12)* —

Ascension is called the forgotten festival because it is often neglected and frequently goes unnoticed even by church members. The same sad title could be given to Epiphany, with perhaps even more reason. Many Christians do not know what the church is celebrating on Epiphany Sunday. Few understand how it could be a source of daily strength for them. Are we any different? Has Epiphany any real meaning for us in our daily needs? Does it make a difference in our lives? Let's look at this festival today.

The dictionary defines *Epiphany* as a kind of manifestation or revelation of Christ's divinity. The texts that have been chosen for the Epiphany season show us unmistakably the true identity of that little child lying in a manger. Throughout the entire Epiphany season, we listen to accounts of the exciting miracles Jesus performed, the signs that pointed to

Jesus as God's Son and our Savior. It is little wonder that these Epiphany texts are treasured and loved by many Christians. But do they have meaning for our lives? Do we walk in the light of Epiphany throughout the year?

It is not by accident that Epiphany is celebrated shortly before Lent. It prepares us to understand both the horror and the glory of Lent. Epiphany texts keep before our eyes the reality that the Christ we see abused, mocked, and crucified was in no way a helpless victim of enemies who were more powerful than he was. He was not a mere man going down to defeat.

Rather, all through the passion story we see that he was the one in control, not his enemies. They carried out his plan, not theirs. See them fall helpless before him in Gethsemane. Listen to him openly identifying himself to them with his words and by his miracle of healing, restoring the ear of the high priest's servant. Notice how easily he protects his disciples with a divine command: "Let these men go" (John 18:8). How astonishing it was that this armed mob should humbly obey their captive!

Epiphany reminds us how effortlessly the Lord of glory could have crushed that multitude, Pilate, and the soldiers nailing him to the cross. So it was not really the nails that held Jesus there. It was his love for his captors and you and me. His cry, "It is finished" (John 19:30), was not a cry of defeat. It was a triumphant battle cry of victory, of completed redemption. Nothing more needed to be done by sinners or for sinners, for in that moment our debt of sin was canceled. We were completely reconciled with God.

Just a little thought will show us how the message of Epiphany and its manifestation of Christ's true glory can help us meet the crosses and trials of our lives. It keeps reminding us who this Jesus in whom we trust really is, and it keeps reminding us what he has done for us. It reassures us that our lives are in the hands of the King of kings who can surely protect us and guide us safely to heaven. With him nothing is too difficult.

He is the Lord, who showed his might by dividing the waters of the Red Sea. He brought water out of dry rock for several million people and their cattle. A thousand or so years later, he turned water into wine, stilled a furious storm, healed countless sick people, raised Lazarus from the dead, and then he himself arose as crowning proof of our redemption.

As we grow older and begin each day with a little less strength, it is of wondrous comfort to know that this Lord is beside us and to know at day's end that he watches over our beds as we sleep. When the psalmist asks, "Who is this King of glory?" we confidently answer with him, "[It is] the LORD strong and mighty, the LORD mighty in battle" (Psalm 24:8). What a Lord he is! What peace fills our hearts as we go through life in the light of Epiphany!

— *Prayer* —

We thank you, dear Lord, for all those miracles—signs pointing to you as the true Savior and Lord. May we walk confidently in the certainty that your Epiphany gives us. Amen.

58

HE SPEAKS TO YOU ABOUT YOU, JESUS, AND GETHSEMANE

"Abba, Father," he said, "everything is possible for you. Take this cup from me. Yet not what I will, but what you will."

— (Mark 14:36) —

A visit to the Garden of Gethsemane will teach us many comforting truths. There we see again the depths of Christ's love, even as he reached out to the betrayer, Judas Iscariot. We catch a glimpse of the depths of his suffering for our sins, as his sweat became as drops of blood. We note how easily he protected his own from an armed mob, how effortlessly he brought them all to the ground at his feet. We hear him identify himself for them and for us. And we hear a beautiful, perfect prayer. Let's listen to the Son of God as he kneels in prayer in Gethsemane and learn from him how to pray.

All those enemies surrounding him and all that suffering that he knew lay ahead did not for a moment shake his faith in his Father's ability to help. Not a shred of doubt does he express about the power of God. Rather, he shows us the perfect trust with which we also want to meet our dark hours.

Powerful forces were arrayed against him, even the prince of darkness, but he was confident that his Father could brush those forces aside like pesky flies. If necessary, the Father could have sent countless angels, one of whom would have been more than enough. Listen as he expresses his faith even now, "*Abba,* Father, everything is possible for you."

Jesus was confident, not only of his Father's power but of his wisdom and love as well. We may know in our hearts that God can heal our illnesses, but what if he decides not to do so? What happens then? Does our faith end there? Look again at Jesus. He has brought his suffering to the one he knew could intervene. Then he simply leaves the issue in his Father's hands: "Take this cup from me. Yet not what I will, but what you will."

Jesus knew that his Father could easily prevent the torture and pain that would be laid upon him on Good Friday, but he also knew that the salvation of the world was at stake. And if his escaping the cross meant risking the plan of redemption, which he had in eternity agreed on with the Father, then the choice was obvious for him because he loved sinners so much. With the words "not my will, but yours be done" (Luke 22:42), he committed all things into the hands of his loving Father. He knew his Father would carry out the only possible plan of salvation, whatever the cost to both of them.

What are the vital elements of this perfect Gethsemane prayer? First, we want to direct our prayers to the one who is almighty, the one who demonstrated his love for us at the cross—that same love in which he may find it necessary for us to suffer for a time. We know that he will not permit us to suffer even one moment of pain unless it is necessary for our eternal welfare. So while we do pray, "If it be possible, . . ." yet we are not suggesting with that expression that somehow or other it may not be possible for God to help us. Rather, using these words suggests that we realize that the cup of suffering may not be avoidable without endangering our eternal future.

Second, "Your will, not mine," we pray, though it is the most difficult of prayers. It implies total submission to God's way and will. Nevertheless, we pray confidently, because we know he will carefully evaluate what we ask and choose the answer that he knows to be best for us.

We don't enjoy suffering, but we know from God's Word that suffering may be what we need at times. Grapes need to be crushed to become wine, a rough diamond must be struck to become beautiful, marble must be chiseled to become a statue, iron needs fire to become steel, and gold needs fire to become pure. So our Father knows exactly what he must do in love for us to keep us his own and bring us to heaven. To that we say, "Amen!"

— Prayer —

**Savior, may your prayer in Gethsemane
teach us to pray as you did there. Let us never
doubt our Father's ability to help and always trust
him to give us what we need, saying with you,
"Not what I will, but what you will." Amen.**

59

HE SPEAKS TO YOU AS YOU STAND BENEATH THE CROSS

"I have been crucified with Christ and I no longer live, but Christ lives in me."

— *(Galatians 2:20)* —

A haunting African-American spiritual directs some pointed questions at us: "Were you there when they crucified my Lord? . . . when they nailed him to the tree? . . . when they laid him in the tomb?" Our answer to those questions will indicate how well we understand what took place at Calvary. Of course we were not there physically, for it took place thousands of miles away and nearly two thousand years ago. However, the real questions asked by that spiritual are these: "Were you and I there in the guilt that made Jesus' suffering necessary? Were our sins the cause of his anguish?"

The world almost shouts its answer: "In no way was I there! I had no part in that crucifixion. It was Caiaphas; it was Pilate; it was the Jewish leaders; it was those Roman soldiers. His own people did it; blame them, not us."

But we can hardly separate ourselves from the atrocities of Calvary if we listen to the writers of Scripture, all of whom not only implicate us, but directly admit that *they* were there—even Isaiah who lived some seven hundred years before the crucifixion took place. He was speaking for them all, for us, and for all the world when he wrote, "He was crushed *for our* iniquities" (53:5) and when he said, "The LORD has laid on him the iniquity of *us all*" (53:6). Paul made the same confession: "God made him who had no sin to be sin for us" (2 Corinthians 5:21). Centuries later a hymn writer expressed it this way: "My burden in your passion, Lord, you have borne for me, For it was my transgression, My shame, on Calvary" (CW 105:4).

The apostle Paul put it bluntly, yet eloquently, "I have been crucified with Christ." How could Paul say that? Quite likely he was nowhere near Calvary on Good Friday! Yet he saw Jesus, as his substitute, in the place where he rightly should have been, nailed to the cross, suffering the agony that was Paul's by right, and dying for him. Paul made no effort to gloss over his part in the crucifixion—his guilt that caused the suffering of Jesus. Paul's theology of the cross was expressed in these simple words: "[He] loved me and gave himself for me" (Galatians 2:20). Yes, Paul says that he was there. To him it was as though he had carried a cross to that awful hill, but just as the nails were about to be driven through his hands and feet, God provided his own Son as a willing substitute for Paul. The scourging and the nails did not touch Paul. All was done to the one who took his place. "[He] gave himself for me."

That tiny word *for* expresses one of the most vital concepts in the Bible—Jesus died for us, that is, in our place, so that we do not need to die for our sins. God found a way to be just and yet not punish sinners. "[God] is faithful and just and will forgive us our sins," John writes (1 John 1:9). Can you imagine the pain this cost our heavenly Father, forsaking and punishing his holy Son *for us?* So we gladly admit that we were there when they crucified our Lord.

When the famous painter Rembrandt wished to confess his part in the crucifixion, he painted his own face on one of the figures in the crowd gathered around the cross. He too was there. He too had helped crucify Jesus.

What a comfort is ours along with a sense of shame! For when Jesus suffered on the cross, in God's eyes we suffered there, we died there, and our debt was finished! Not with reluctance, then, but eagerly and anxiously we shout our answer to the hymn, "Yes, I was there!"

And because he endured it all for my sin and in my place, I need not suffer or fear being forsaken. Because he died for me, I am done with death.

Were you there when they crucified your Lord? Thank God you were. You were involved in that payment for all your sin. May that be your comfort and peace in living and dying.

— *Prayer* —

How can we ever thank you, loving Savior, for the way of sorrows that took you to the cross in our place. There you suffered what we had earned by our sin. There you were forsaken that we need never be. There you died that we might live. Thank you, Lord Jesus. Amen.

60

HE SPEAKS TO YOU ABOUT EASTER IN YOUR HEART

Remember Jesus Christ, raised from the dead,
descended from David. This is my gospel.

— *(2 Timothy 2:8)* —

We can hardly forget the Easter services in our churches—the filled pews, the triumphant hymns, the powerful resurrection sermons. They are thrilling and unforgettable.

Yet at times we act as if we've forgotten Easter—we act as though we waved good-bye to the angels at the tomb and left their triumphant message behind for another year. We act as though we're disturbed and troubled with the same old doubts and fears that the Lord's resurrection should have banished once and for all.

We are, of course, absolutely convinced that Jesus did arise and is alive and is with us every moment. Yet, we manage somehow to have days when we forget and give the impression, with our pessimism and gloom, that he is still in that tomb. Is the Sunday after Easter in your church, for example, too often "low Sunday"—low in enthusiasm, low in attendance, low in joy and hope? How can we soar on one

Sunday like eagles on wings of faith and so soon flounder on broken wings?

The apostle Paul felt the need to warn us against the danger of forgetting Easter. "Remember Jesus Christ, raised from the dead." Remember the message of that empty tomb. It certifies that Jesus is truly risen and is God's Son, nailing down the truth of every word and promise of his and the fulfillment of our redemption. It assures us that because he lives, we too shall live. These vital truths have all been established by the Easter event, and it remains only that we now apply these truths to every moment of our lives.

To do that was difficult even for the disciples who were there! Early Easter morning those faithful women were on their way to the tomb, carrying embalming spices. They were clearly not on their way to a joyful Easter sunrise service! With their faces masked in gloom, they were carrying preparations for a dead Christ. Even at the empty tomb, "trembling and bewildered, the women went out and fled from the tomb" (Mark 16:8).

Easter evening saw all of the disciples, except Thomas, hidden behind locked doors—in fear, without Easter courage. In fact, all that day the disciples had lived in the gloom of Good Friday, frightened and hopeless and sad. That was certainly not remembering and living by the Easter promise Christ had given them.

Only gradually did the Easter sun shine into their hearts. "The disciples were overjoyed when they saw the Lord" (John 20:20). Suddenly they were transformed into new creatures, filled with peace and joy and courage that nothing could shake. Every day was touched and brightened by the Easter sun. Every Sunday became an Easter celebration. Every sermon became a resurrection message.

This is how we apply Easter to our daily lives, living as though Jesus had risen this very day before our eyes.

Easter must not become for us an island to which we travel once a year to celebrate Christ's rising and then leave it behind for the next 364 days. Easter is the mainland on which we want to live all year, walking with the risen Lord.

After a life of incredible sadness, Easter enabled Paul Gerhardt to write: "This is a sight that gladdens—What peace it does impart! Now nothing ever saddens The joy within my heart. No gloom shall ever shake, No foe shall ever take The hope which God's own Son In love for me has won" (CW 156:3).

Let Easter be a mighty fact in your life. Jesus lives! "He lives to silence all my fears. He lives to wipe away my tears. Oh, the sweet joy this sentence gives: 'I know that my Redeemer lives!'" (CW 152:5,8).

— *Prayer* —

Lord Jesus, as we today gather before your empty tomb, our hearts overflow with peace and joy. We rejoice in you, our living Savior. May the Easter sun shine into every dark corner of our hearts and give us the joy that nothing can touch. Amen.

61

HE SPEAKS TO YOU WALKING WITH YOUR ASCENDED LORD

He was taken up before their very eyes,
and a cloud hid him from their sight.

— *(Acts 1:9)* —

The world pays no attention to Ascension Day. It is business as usual. Even for Christians, the day does not have the excitement of Christmas or Easter. Actually this forgotten festival is a very significant day for us. Let's think about its consequences for a moment.

Like Good Friday, the day of Christ's ascension could have been a very sad and frightening one for the disciples. Their best friend, the one in whom they had always found refuge, was leaving them, not for just another town in Palestine, but for his home in heaven. No longer would they be able to run to him with questions or problems. No longer could they seek his protection and comfort. They would see no more miracles and hear no more words of his.

How meaningful to us was their reaction when "a cloud hid him from their sight." Not the fear or despair that one might expect, but absolute trust! "They . . . returned to

Jerusalem with great joy!" (Luke 24:52). Even without Jesus beside them, they returned now unafraid to the very stronghold of those enemies who had crucified Jesus and who might well have been seeking them for the same purpose. Notice how they went: boldly, not timidly; joyfully, not sadly.

Parting is painful. How then can we explain their actions? Didn't they even care that Jesus had left them? Weren't they feeling abandoned and on their own? How can it be that they returned with great joy?

The answer shows that we have no less reason to leave every Ascension Day service with that same joy and boldness, even if we are returning to a life of danger and trouble. Christ's ascension is all positive news for those who belong to Jesus. His ascension was an announcement that he had completed his work on earth. He had reconciled people with God, and they now had peace with the Father through faith in Christ.

Furthermore, Jesus did not just disappear. The disciples saw where he was going. They saw him returning in triumph to his heavenly Father and ours. He was about to be crowned as King of kings and Lord of lords according to his human nature also. God was placing all things under his feet to be ruled by him.

And—this is an exciting truth—as King of kings and Lord of lords, he rules over all things for his people. In Ephesians 1:22, we are told, "God placed all things under his feet and appointed him to be head over everything *for* the church." Whatever happens in the world, wherever it happens, and whenever it happens, the Lord is controlling it for the welfare of his people—for us.

Jesus was not really leaving his own behind. In fact, he left with an act of blessing that continues to bless us and with a promise that still stands: "Surely I am with you always, to the very end of the age" (Matthew 28:20). He left with a promise that assured us that all power was given to him over all things in heaven and on earth. In that power he rules and acts on behalf of his beloved. And in heaven, he is interceding for us when we sin. His nail-pierced hands provide the evidence that our debt of sin is paid in full. Even our physical separation from him is only temporary, for he is preparing a place for us and is coming to take us there to be with him forever. With him! At his throne! Ruling with him! That is how the ascension story will end for us: forever with the Lord.

Are you walking with your ascended Lord today? Thank God you are!

— *Prayer* —

*May your ascension, Lord, fill us with
fresh courage in the certainty that you walk with
us every day and that one day you will return to take
us home forever. How we look forward to that joyous
family reunion with you and all the saints! Amen.*

Sixteen

62

HE SPEAKS TO YOU ABOUT HIS PENTECOST BLESSINGS

*All of them were filled with the Holy Spirit
and began to speak in other tongues
as the Spirit enabled them.*

— (Acts 2:4) —

You know that astonishing wonders basic to your salvation took place on that first Christian Pentecost Sunday. You remember those wonders—the sound of the mighty, rushing wind that drew people to the scene, the forked tongues of fire on the heads of the disciples, the strange ability of unlearned disciples to speak in foreign languages, their bold courage to witness of the crucified Savior, their suddenly clear perception of God's truth, and the miraculous conversions of thousands. Indeed, what day could claim more wonders than Pentecost?

But what have those wonders to do with us almost two thousand years later? Just how do they enrich our lives? It helps to know about the wonders that were worked by the Holy Spirit that day, because the same blessings of Pentecost are ours. The same Holy Spirit, who gave bolder faith and courage and clearer understanding to the disciples, who turned the lives of three thousand completely around so that they suddenly loved the Savior they had hated, is still with us to work the same wonders in our hearts.

We've already experienced the greatest of them, for he kindled the spark of saving faith in our dead hearts at our baptisms. He opened our eyes to see the beauty of a Savior slain for us. He is still using the same power tools, the Word and sacraments, to work the same wonders for us that so enriched thousands that day. He makes our faith grow. He enlightens us with more and more knowledge of God. He enables us to lead holier lives. He keeps us in Christ, doing all this, as Luther put it, daily and richly. He works in us every time we use the Word of God and the sacraments.

God lists the wonders and wonderful gifts of the Holy Spirit in Galatians 5:22,23: "The fruit of the Spirit is love, joy, peace, patience, kindness, goodness, faithfulness, gentleness and self-control."

Unlike the world, which cares nothing about these gifts, we have learned to cherish the Holy Spirit and his work in us. And the older we get and the longer we live, the more important they become to us. We find ourselves drawing closer to that appointment with God when nothing matters but what the Holy Spirit alone can do for us. Because of him we became, and still are, God's redeemed children by faith in Jesus, cleansed of sin and sure of heaven.

In a very real sense, we Christians are wonders worked by the Holy Spirit—his workmanship. He sought us out and worked his wonders in our hearts as he did in Paul and in the dying thief, as he has done in every child of God. He worked one of the greatest wonders of Christmas when he brought Mary to believe that her helpless child was her Creator, her God, and her Redeemer. From him, we too have the precious gift of faith that makes us God's children.

The older we get, the more we cherish the gifts of the Holy Spirit that enable us to stand before God's throne as his redeemed ones. The older we get, the more often our prayers are directed to him to keep us safe to that day.

"Holy Spirit, Light divine, Shine upon this heart of mine; Chase the gloom of night away; Turn the darkness into day" (CW 183:1).

— *Prayer* —

Dear Holy Spirit, may we treasure your Word and sacraments, the power tools by which you work wonders in our hearts and prepare us for our eternal home. Amen.

63

HE SPEAKS TO YOU ABOUT DREAMING OF HEAVEN

For here we do not have an enduring city,
but we are looking for the city that is to come.

— *(Hebrews 13:14)* —

When people are young and healthy, they may go for months without giving heaven a second thought. At the time it seems so far away and almost irrelevant. That changes drastically, however, when we lose someone very close to us, or when our own death seems near. Suddenly the thought of heaven and eternity takes center stage in our hearts and minds. Do those thoughts fill us with apprehension or with eager anticipation?

What will heaven be like? Let's listen as God tells us a few things about his home, our future address. Though we may dream about heaven, it is not just a dream or some sort of vision. It is a reality, a very real place—a place of perfect peace and glory and joy. God describes its splendor and beauty and speaks of it as his home. How could it be anything else but glorious?

God has not told us directly where heaven is, but many Bible passages cause us to think of heaven as far above us. It is where our Lord went when he ascended. It is called God's home, so he is there, as are all the angels.

Also there at this very moment are all those who from the beginning died in the Lord—died believing in him. There is no long wait, no "soul sleep," for Jesus said to the dying thief, "*Today* you will be with me in paradise," (Luke 23:43), and again later he said, "Blessed are the dead who die in the Lord *from now on*" (Revelation 14:13). While we struggle with life's disappointments and miseries, they are already drinking of the river of God's delights forever (Psalm 36:8).

Will we recognize our loved ones? God has revealed to us that we will have the same bodies, but they will be perfect like that of the risen Lord, for "we shall be like him" (1 John 3:2). We will no longer be subject to pain, weakness, deformity, and misery. We will have the *same bodies*. God says so. We will indeed recognize our parents and friends and families, as well as the saints we have met in the pages of Scripture.

What about those close to us who did not die in the Lord? Will not their absence in heaven dampen and spoil our joy? There is no grief in heaven, and because our will shall totally conform with God's, we will know no regret.

When will our joy begin? Since we will be a part of the harvest safely gathered in forever, Isaiah could speak of everlasting joy and gladness (Isaiah 35:10) that begins for us in the moment of death. "Our mouths," says the psalmist, will be "filled with laughter, our tongues with songs of joy" (Psalm 126:2). No gloom ever again—only unspoiled and unending joy, seeing Jesus face-to-face, wearing a crown of glory indicating both victory and honor in belonging to the Lord.

All the unbelievably exciting truths God tells us about his heaven would be quite meaningless if they were clouded with uncertainty as to whether we, as unworthy sinners, would even deserve to be there. But we will be there as God's saints entirely by his grace. Our salvation—our being there in heaven—is entirely *his* doing, done out of pure grace.

Nothing depends on us, not even our faith in Jesus, which is the gift of the Holy Spirit. He made us his own. He has kept us as his own, so we *know* we will be there one day, perhaps very soon. (We can't get there too soon!)

We have in no way covered all that God has revealed to us about what is to be our permanent address, but we know enough to be filled with homesickness and longing and anticipation. There *is* a heaven, a place of peace and joy, where Jesus and our loved ones are waiting. "And so we will be with the Lord forever" (1 Thessalonians 4:17).

What a future we have! Think of it often when your spirits are down.

— *Prayer* —

*Lord and Savior, may our eyes ever
look beyond the things that are temporary
to the home you have prepared for us,
where we will be with you forever. Amen.*

64

HE SPEAKS TO YOU AS YOU AWAIT THE LORD'S RETURN

Now, dear children, continue in him, so that when he appears we may be confident and unashamed before him at his coming.

— (1 John 2:28) —

Jesus is coming! If only one line or one word of Scripture reported that event, that would be sufficient. Actually, however, Jesus and the prophets and apostles speak of it over and over again in the Bible. Jesus has not revealed the date of his return, since he wants us to be ready for his coming at any time; but he has given us many signs, which will precede his coming, to remind us that the day is surely drawing near. As we see those signs multiplying all around us, our hearts are filled with excitement and anticipation for that great day.

Yes, he is coming, perhaps soon, perhaps this very day. The question we should be asking ourselves every day is whether we are ready or not. His return is certainly the most significant event still remaining on the world's calendar. Nothing even begins to compare with it in importance—not a war, not a depression, nothing in our personal lives. At the

198

moment that he comes, *everything else* will become totally irrelevant and meaningless—our jobs, our homes, our health, our bank accounts. The big question is this: Is my house in order?

You may have read the story of the rich landowner who left his servants in charge of his huge estate when he set off on a long journey. Time passed. Much later a visitor arrived at the estate. Knowing how long the owner had already been absent, he was amazed to find everyone so busy and the place in such perfect condition. He asked one of the servants: "How can this be? You are doing your work as though your master were returning tomorrow!" The servant replied, "No, sir, not tomorrow, today!"

If our Lord were to return today, would he find us busy at the work he has given us? Will we be ready, whenever he chooses to return?

Even a casual glance at the lives we are living could cause us serious misgivings, for we are sinning every day. Yet, amazingly, there is no terror in our hearts and no apprehension. Rather there is boldness and eagerness. To illustrate, let me tell you about a personal experience. Once in a most vivid dream, I saw the Lord return in an unbelievable blaze of glory, surrounded by countless angels. Though it was an awesome sight, a sight to fill one with awe, my first thought was "Why, I'm not afraid!"

The dream dramatized the reality that we can boldly lift up our heads to greet the Lord at his coming. God himself assures us of that in his Word. John in our text reminds us that as we abide in Jesus, putting our trust in him, when he shall appear, we may have boldness and not be ashamed before him at his coming. (See 1 John 4:17 also.)

What unbelievably good news this is for us! Even though we daily sin often, we need not be ashamed before him at his coming. Our record of sin has been erased, wiped clean through the holy, precious blood of Jesus. Yes, we have broken God's commandments, but Paul assures us, "You were washed, you were sanctified, you were justified in the name of the Lord Jesus Christ and by the Spirit of our God" (1 Corinthians 6:11). Again he tells us, "Therefore, there is now no condemnation for those who are in Christ Jesus" (Romans 8:1). No matter how black our record, "though [our] sins are like scarlet, they shall be as white as snow; though they are red as crimson, they shall be like wool" (Isaiah 1:18).

This will make us bold at his coming. We will lift up our heads with joy, confident of standing before God as though we had never sinned. We are ready!

Above my desk is a little reminder: "Perhaps today!" It is a happy, welcome sign! Let it be today; it can't happen too soon. Come, Lord Jesus!

— *Prayer* —

Come, Lord Jesus.
Come quickly. Amen.

65

HE SPEAKS TO YOU AS YOU GET READY FOR ANYTHING

We know that in all things God works for the good of those who love him, who have been called according to his purpose.

— *(Romans 8:28)* —

We have come to the last pages of this humble book in which God has spoken us in our many different needs and situations. In a sense, we have used a lot of words when four would have been sufficient. The entire content of this book could have been written on one page or in one line of four little words that cover every situation—four words that speak to every condition the elderly may encounter. You know those words and have often turned to the comfort they offer: *all things for good.*

In these devotions, we have surely missed some situations that may touch your life, but that does not matter. Every situation is covered by that astonishing phrase. All those situations are directed and controlled by the same love that gave us Good Friday and Easter and still surrounds us like a warm blanket today. These four words deserve a closer look.

Paul begins by saying "We know"—not we imagine, we think, we are fairly certain. There is no question about it. Moreover, he leaves no room for any exceptions. He does not say "in many things" or even "in most things" but "in *all* things," in whatever happens.

Does that include the mistakes we make? Yes, the Lord can turn them around and make them serve our good. Even our sins? We deeply regret them, but knowing that they have all been mercifully forgiven, we are, as a result, filled with a greater awareness of the danger of temptation. We have a greater reverence and awe before God's forgiving mercy, a greater thankfulness for what God has done for us, a greater desire to live in a way that shows our gratitude, and a greater certainty that God also overrides the purposes of our enemies.

Just imagine, all things for good. The worst calamities that threaten to crush us, the most bitter disappointments—all must surrender to these four little words. So must the little, trivial irritations that frustrate us. God is there to work out his purpose. He has a plan for our lives, and that is all we need to know. He gives us these four words to arm us for any situation. We want to memorize and carry them with us every day.

Jesus tells us that what he is now doing we may not understand, but the day is coming when we will. Sometimes we don't have to wait, for what at first look like tragedies immediately turn out for the best. One door to opportunity closes, and another opens to something better. A family that missed a plane flight later learns that the plane crashed. The world calls this good luck. We Christians see God's hand at work.

But we must recognize that God has a higher goal in mind for us than today's happiness or success. He who owns all things could make us all billionaires and not be one bit the poorer for it. He could make all of us robustly healthy every day of our lives, for he is more powerful than any disease. But he has a higher good in mind, an eternal good. What happens to us in the end is what counts with him. Whatever takes place in our lives is drawing us closer to him and our real goal.

It grieves the Savior to see us sad even for a moment, but because he loves us, *he must* at times take from us that which we consider so important because it threatens our goal. He may have to put us flat on our backs in order for us to see how helpless we are without him and how much we need him or to recognize how meaningless the whole world is unless we have him. The end result will always be the same— all things for good—the good that is his loving purpose for us.

We hope that these final pages are a summary of what God says to us all. Take these words with you—all things for good—and you will be hopeful and contented and secure. You will, indeed, be ready for anything. That is our fervent prayer for you.

— *Prayer* —

*All things for good! Oh, what confidence and hope
these four little words give us. May the Holy Spirit
write them on our hearts and give us faith to face
every danger and need, in the sure hope
they offer and work in us. Amen.*